'Woven through this uniqu[e volume is the idea that] research methodologies can n[ot be developed in a] vacuum. Instead, validity eme[rges from the] relations of power, agency, and identity [among] diverse actors. The original insights generated by the chapter authors in discussing their research attest to the important contribution this volume makes to our understanding of the nature of scientific inquiry.'

Professor Emeritus Jim Cummins, Ontario Institute for Studies in Education, University of Toronto

'This is a superb and timely book given the increasing ethnic and cultural diversity within society. It provides an excellent framework for researchers from the 'hegemonic mainstream' to examine and respond to the multiple dimensions of power evident when planning and conducting research involving participants from ethnic- and linguistic-minority backgrounds.'

Professor Vini Lander, Faculty of Education, Edge Hill University, UK

'A fascinating collection of research about social justice in education. These chapters, based in a diversity of settings, show new ways of accessing and sharing the experiences of minority students and teachers that minimize distortion, are respectful, and actively empower.'

Dr Terry Wrigley, Visiting Professor, Leeds Metropolitan University

Methodologies for Researching Cultural Diversity in Education

IOEPress Trentham Books

Methodologies for Researching Cultural Diversity in Education

International perspectives

Edited by Geri Smyth and Ninetta Santoro

A Trentham Book
Institute of Education Press

First published in 2014 by the Institute of Education, University of London,
20 Bedford Way, London WC1H 0AL
ioepress.co.uk

© Geri Smyth and Ninetta Santoro 2015

British Library Cataloguing in Publication Data:
A catalogue record for this publication is available from the British Library

ISBNs
978-1-85856-523-1 (paperback)
978-1-85856-631-3 (PDF eBook)
978-1-85856-632-0 (ePub eBook)
978-1-85856-633-7 (Kindle eBook)

All rights reserved. No part of this publication may be reproduced, stored in a retrieval system, or transmitted in any form or by any means, electronic, mechanical, photocopying, recording, or otherwise, without the prior permission of the copyright owner.

Every effort has been made to trace copyright holders and to obtain their permission for the use of copyright material. The publisher apologizes for any errors or omissions and would be grateful if notified of any corrections that should be incorporated in future reprints or editions of this book.

The opinions expressed in this publication are those of the authors and do not necessarily reflect the views of the Institute of Education, University of London.

Typeset by Quadrant Infotech (India) Pvt Ltd
Printed by CPI Group (UK) Ltd, Croydon CR0 4YY

Cover images, clockwise from top left: ©iStock.com/CEFutcher; ©iStock.com/skynesher; ©iStock.com/AmmentorpDK; ©iStock.com/CEFutcher

Contents

About the authors   viii

Introduction   xii

1. Discursive shadowing as a methodological approach in a study of bilingual teachers
   Joke Dewilde   1

2. Power and knowledge in research with immigrant teachers: Questioning the insider/outsider dichotomy
   Clea Schmidt   14

3. Unsettling truths: Post-structural ethnography as a tool to trouble schooling exclusions
   Kathryn Edgeworth   26

4. Being a socio-professional insider-researcher in Pakistan: Possibilities and challenges for educational research
   Saeeda Shah   42

5. Overcoming barriers in researching diversity
   Geri Smyth   58

6. Researcher as cartographer: Mapping the experiences of culturally diverse research participants
   Ninetta Santoro   74

7. Participatory action research in a high school drama club: A catalyst for change among English Language Learners in Canada
   Antoinette Gagné and Stephanie Soto Gordon   91

8. Children's agency in research: Does photography empower participants?
   Giovanna Fassetta   106

Index   122

About the authors

Geri Smyth holds a Chair in Education at the University of Strathclyde in Scotland, where she is also Director of Research in the School of Education. She has over 20 years' experience in the preparation of teachers for multilingual and multicultural classrooms and the supervision of doctoral students working in related fields. She provides in-service education internationally on teaching in multilingual classrooms and on culturally responsive research. Her research is predominantly ethnographic and utilizes methodologies designed particularly to give voice to respondents of diverse linguistic backgrounds. Smyth has published widely in the areas of bilingual education, diversity in the teaching profession and refugee studies. She has been co-editor of the *European Journal of Teacher Education* since 2008.

Ninetta Santoro has recently taken up a Chair in Education at the University of Strathclyde in Scotland, having previously been a Professor of Education and the Head of the School of Teacher Education at Charles Sturt University, Australia. She has been a teacher educator for 20 years and has extensive experience in initial teacher education programmes and as a doctoral supervisor. Her work draws on theories of post-structuralism to examine teacher and student ethnicity and how these positionings shape teaching and learning; the preparation of teachers for ethnically diverse contexts; and internationalization. Santoro has been the recipient of several major research grants and has published widely in the areas of race and ethnicity, teacher education, culturally diverse learners and qualitative research methodologies. She was a co-editor of the *Asia-Pacific Journal of Teacher Education* between 2008 and 2013. She is currently an Adjunct Professor at Charles Sturt University, Australia.

Joke Dewilde holds a position as Associate Professor in Education at Hedmark University College, Norway, where she is also Director of Studies for the teacher education programme for bilingual teachers. As a teacher educator and supervisor of students, she is particularly engaged in issues related to the fields of multilingualism and multilingual education. In her PhD dissertation, Dewilde was concerned with the opportunities and challenges bilingual migrant teachers encounter in Norwegian compulsory schools. In her research more generally, she combines ethnographic methods with interaction analysis, thus aiming at the development of participant-sensitive methods. She has been an active member of the research group Education and Diversity at Hedmark University College since 2006.

Clea Schmidt is an Associate Professor of Teaching English as an Additional Language in the Faculty of Education at the University of Manitoba. She served as founding coordinator of the Academic and Professional Bridging Program for Internationally Educated Teachers (IETs) and the IET Mentorship Initiative from 2005 to 2011. Her scholarly interests include advocacy and research related to equity for culturally and linguistically diverse teachers and learners. Schmidt conducts mixed methods and qualitative research informed by critical theory. Regional, national, and international projects have included the evaluation of a programme designed to embed the Essential Skills in lower-level Canadian Language Benchmarks classes, assessment of school division responses to learners and families for whom English is an Additional Language, and barriers to the integration of internationally educated teachers. She recently co-edited a volume published by Trentham entitled *Learning Spaces for Social Justice: International perspectives on exemplary practices from preschool to secondary school*.

Kathryn Edgeworth is a Lecturer in the Faculty of Education, University of Tasmania, Australia, where she teaches humanities and social sciences. Prior to that she practised as a secondary school teacher in rural and remote Australia for ten years. She earned her doctorate in the sociology of education from Charles Sturt University in 2012. Her thesis explored the lived experience of ethnic minority, Muslim and refugee students in rural schools. She has a particular research interest in pedagogies that trouble schooling exclusions for ethnic and religious minority students. Edgeworth has published in the areas of post-structural research methodologies, ethnic and cultural diversity, social justice, and rural education and schooling. She joined the editorial board of *The Social Educator* in 2014.

Saeeda Shah is a Reader in Education at the School of Education, University of Leicester. She is also Visiting Professor of Education at the University of Derby. She previously worked in higher education in Pakistan,

Edited by Geri Smyth and Ninetta Santoro

holding senior leadership positions with both academic and administrative responsibilities. Her research interests include educational leadership with a focus on Muslim education, Islamic philosophy of education, and gender and power issues. Shah has published in the areas of education of Muslims, leadership, Islam and society, gender, diversity, inclusion, and identity/ethnicity. She has presented her work at international conferences in many parts of the world and is recognized as an international authority in her field of expertise. She has also been actively involved in the voluntary sector in Britain since 1995, and has participated in the United Nations Human Rights Commission's sessions, particularly in relation to the rights of women and youth.

Antoinette Gagné is an Associate Professor at the Ontario Institute of Studies in Education (OISE) of the University of Toronto. She has over 30 years' experience in preparing teachers to work with diverse students and has supervised the research of doctoral students in related fields. As Academic Advisor for the OISE Student Success Centre from 2005 onward, she has worked closely with a team of doctoral candidates to meet the academic and cultural needs of undergraduate and graduate students in education. Gagné is also involved in research with immigrant teachers and learners and has explored the use of innovative qualitative methodologies designed to give voice to diverse participants. She has written extensively about diversity issues in education and the experiences of immigrant children, teachers and families in the Canadian education system.

Stephanie Soto Gordon is an English as a Second Language (ESL) teacher at William Lyon Mackenzie Collegiate Institute, Toronto District School Board, a field partner with Ontario Institute of Studies in Education, University of Toronto, and an ESL communication consultant. Her research interests include identity, motivation, second language education, teacher education, social justice and equity.

Giovanna Fassetta has over 20 years' experience as a teacher, having worked in Italy, Eritrea and the UK. In 2012 she was awarded a PhD in sociology from the University of Strathclyde, Scotland, for a thesis on migrant children's expectations and experiences of life in Italy. Her research interests are children's perspectives on migration; diversity in education; intersectionality; and the use of participatory methodologies and visual techniques in particular. Since gaining her doctorate, Fassetta has undertaken further social and educational inquiry into migration issues in her capacity as a Research Associate at the University of Strathclyde. Her interest in migration and human rights also includes her volunteer work with Scottish Detainee Visitors, a charity that offers emotional and practical support to migrants detained in Dungavel Immigration Removal Centre, Scotland.

Introduction

This book is about the conduct of educational research in culturally diverse contexts. While cultural and ethnic diversity has always been present in just about all societies, its impact on teaching and learning has not always been acknowledged or understood. However, in an increasingly globalized world where levels of national border crossing and migration – both voluntary and forced – are at unprecedented levels, cultural and ethnic diversity cannot be ignored. Nations that may once have considered their populations to be culturally homogenous and unified are now regarding their national identities as multiple, complex and changeable. Even in nations that have always been characterized by high levels of cultural diversity, such as Australia, Canada and North America, the nature of their diversity is changing in response to periods of political upheaval and war in many regions of the world, as well as the development of global labour and education markets.

These rich and socially complex contexts have important implications for schooling systems, teaching and learning. The requirement to address the needs of students from cultures different from the dominant majority is increasingly the concern of teachers, education policymakers and school management in many parts of the world. Teacher standards in many jurisdictions specify the skills and knowledge teachers need in order to work productively with culturally diverse students. This expectation in turn affects initial teacher education curricula as well as continuing professional development programmes for teachers. The nature of school curricula, pedagogy, assessment and home–school relationships are scrutinized for their potential to enhance the learning experiences of students who bring to their learning a set of cultural practices, knowledge expectations and home languages that differ from those of students from the dominant cultural majority.

Researchers and users of research need to understand the complexity of research in culturally diverse education contexts. The relationship between researched and researcher is of prime importance, and is also potentially particularly problematic. In most cases, researchers are drawn from the hegemonic cultural mainstream and are therefore positioned outside the minority ethnic groups and the experiences they aspire to understand. What is of interest from a research perspective – that is, culture and ethnicity – is also what constitutes a significant point of difference between researchers and their respondents (Santoro and Smyth, 2010). Their position as cultural outsiders to the areas in which they research can raise numerous ethical and methodological issues.

The book

This collection is derived from ongoing work by the Education for Equity and Social Justice research group of the Association for Teacher Education in Europe, which has been discussing issues of culturally and linguistically appropriate research methodologies for some years. The contributors highlight the challenges of researching in culturally and ethnically diverse contexts, bringing together work conducted in Scotland, Australia, Canada, Norway, Italy, Ghana and Pakistan.

In the first chapter Joke Dewilde describes the methodology she developed, which she calls 'Discursive Shadowing'. Dewilde used this approach to undertake ethnographic work with linguistic and ethnic minority teachers in Norwegian schools. This approach was used over an extended period of time and entailed close participant observation and audio recordings of conversations and joint reflections. She argues that it enabled rich and meaningful data to be gathered in a context where the voice of the researched was often marginalized. The teachers with whom Dewilde conducted the research were employed as peripatetic bilingual teachers and the methodology adopted enabled her to access the complexity of their working lives and working relationships and to take a broad view of the concept of teacher collaboration that she was researching. Dewilde demonstrates how this discursive shadowing approach can be particularly useful in contexts characterized by movement, in this case across schools and classrooms.

In chapter 2 Clea Schmidt describes a critical participatory action research project she conducted that investigated six immigrant teachers' experiences in Canadian schools. She focuses not on the research findings, but rather on insights she gleaned from the process of conducting the collaborative research. Framed within a critical theoretical lens, she analyses the relevance of this methodology for scholarship conducted with marginalized groups in education. Working *with* the teachers who were actively involved in designing various aspects of the study, Schmidt suggests that critical participatory action research has the potential to give genuine voice to research participants from marginalized groups and can challenge conventional understandings of who owns and enacts the research agendas, and whose knowledge is valid. The second part of the chapter is a critique of ethics guidelines from a Canadian university. Schmidt highlights the ways in which ethics committees have the potential, through a narrowly defined view of what constitutes 'good' research, to discourage participatory action research. This therefore discriminates against the very research that can eliminate asymmetrical power relationships between researchers and culturally diverse research participants.

In chapter 3, Kathryn Edgeworth discusses the value of post-structural ethnography to research in culturally diverse contexts. She draws on a study she conducted in rural Australia that investigated how students of ethnic and religious minority backgrounds were produced through relations of power and discourses of schooling. She explains the methodological characteristics of post-structural ethnography and presents vignettes of data from two students. Edgeworth argues the value of post-structural ethnography as a tool to unsettle schooling exclusions because it has the potential to facilitate detailed and fine-grained study of the complexities of difference.

Saeeda Shah is concerned with the complexities of insider research. In chapter 4 she raises the questions of who is an insider and under what conditions. She draws on her experience as a researcher in Pakistan, a social context of which she has particular insider knowledge, to bring to our attention the possibility that one can be both an insider and an outsider at the same time. She raises issues of gender, social class and relationships of power in terms of a researcher's ability to access the field, establish relationships and collect data. Shah highlights how being what she describes as a 'socio-professional insider' has implications for data analysis.

In chapter 5, Geri Smyth describes three research projects conducted in Scotland with diverse communities. Though the projects differed in their timescales and respondents, they were connected by methodologies aimed at enabling voices that are often silenced in education to be heard so they could influence educational practices. Through discussion of the approaches used in each project with linguistically and ethnically diverse teachers and learners, Smyth develops an argument for transformative methodologies that will empower diverse participants. The approach offered is drawn from Cummins's model for collaborative empowerment in education through pedagogical choices (2000).

Introduction

In chapter 6, Ninetta Santoro presents the method of analysis she used for the examination of longitudinal interview data from a case study that investigated the experiences and career pathways of newly graduated Indigenous teachers in Australian schools over a three-year period. She describes the characteristics of Situational Analysis, an extension of grounded theory that seeks to make explicit the range of human and non-human contextual factors that have an impact on the situation under analysis. Santoro then presents the step-by-step process she used to construct data maps from the six interviews conducted with one participant over a three-year period. She concludes by arguing that Situational Analysis is useful for researchers working in culturally diverse contexts because it makes visible what might normally be beyond a researcher's field of vision. Those who research within culturally diverse sites where they are cultural outsiders are constantly challenged to find ways of understanding lives and contexts shaped by cultures they are unfamiliar with. Situational Analysis has the potential to raise researchers' awareness of the need for reflective and reflexive research processes that encourage them to consider how they favour certain interpretations over others.

Chapter 7 is a contribution from collaborating researchers in Canada, Antoinette Gagné and Stephanie Soto Gordon. They write about the experience of conducting research in linguistically and culturally diverse secondary schools where the students were given the opportunity to become action researchers and investigate their cross-cultural interactions through making a series of DVDs. The researchers worked with the students to prepare short narratives focusing on the challenges they had faced at school or elsewhere and how they had worked through them to achieve a positive outcome. Using some guiding questions, students were invited to reflect on their own immigration and integration experiences and share their experiences with the other participants. The authors argue that the action research approach allowed them to honour the students' opinions and to minimize the power imbalance that might otherwise have existed.

In the final chapter Giovanna Fassetta discusses the use of photography to collect data with school pupils in Italy and Ghana. The research was investigating children's imaginings and realities of the migration experience and Fassetta chose to use child-led photography so that the children could be engaged directly in the data collection and thus be involved as co-researchers and knowledge-makers. Fassetta takes a reflexive look at her chosen methodology to consider the dynamics and processes that may influence children's choices of subject when using a camera in a research context, and considers the positive aspects of the technique when working with linguistic and ethnic minority participants, suggesting ways to maximize its potential.

References
Santoro, N. and Smyth, G. (2010) 'Researching ethnic "others": conducting critical ethnographic research in Australia and Scotland'. *Intercultural Education*, 21 (6), 493–503.
Cummins, J. (2000) *Language, Power, and Pedagogy: Bilingual children in the crossfire*. Clevedon, UK, and Buffalo, NY: Multilingual Matters.

Chapter 1
Discursive shadowing as a methodological approach in a study of bilingual teachers
Joke Dewilde

Introduction

This chapter discusses an approach called 'discursive shadowing' and its use in studying bilingual teachers in Norwegian schools. Discursive shadowing entails the study of individuals over a period of time by means of participant observation and audio recordings. I argue that this approach can provide a deepened understanding of the complexities of bilingual teachers' working lives. Drawing on the case of a bilingual teacher, Mohammed, at a lower secondary school called Ullstad, one of two studies from my PhD project, I describe how a combination of joint movement, common reflection and ubiquitous recordings elicited rich data that gave new insights into the challenges, problems and opportunities of the teacher's everyday working life.[1]

Being on the move is characteristic of many bilingual teachers' working situations in a Norwegian educational context. Valenta calls them 'travelling teachers', since many bilingual teachers travel between several schools, attending to the needs of a small number of students in each school (2009: 32). In addition, they are, to a greater degree than other teachers, found to ambulate within one school, that is, between classrooms, team rooms and group rooms, and in a more figurative sense between grades, subjects, languages and cultures (Dewilde, 2013).[2] In order to engage with their travelling, I developed a discursive shadowing technique that enabled me to move with the teachers across school settings (hence 'shadowing'), audio record their conversations with others (hence 'discursive'), and reflect upon their work while on the move.

When I suggest discursive shadowing as a suitable methodology for studying bilingual teachers in linguistically, ethnically and cultural diverse contexts, I am not saying that this method cannot be used to gain a deeper understanding of other aspects of diversity, such as age, physical ability, political beliefs, religious beliefs, ethnicity or socio-economic status. Nor does it mean that discursive shadowing is better adapted for studying diverse contexts than other methodologies, as the contributions to this book illustrate, but rather that it creates different possibilities, different insights, tells different stories and hence produces different knowledge, typically with a qualitative stance (Denzin and Lincoln, 2011: 6). As my analyses show, the opportunities created by discursive shadowing in this diverse context also present certain challenges.

I begin by describing the Norwegian context in which my study was conducted, before focusing on the case of Mohammed at Ullstad. When planning the study I realized the need to move around with the bilingual teachers, as well as the importance of translating their conversations in languages I do not know. A brief discussion of shadowing as a research technique is followed by an account of the methodological possibilities and related ethical challenges in using discursive shadowing in a linguistically, ethnically and culturally diverse school setting. In conclusion, I sum up the opportunities and challenges of discursive shadowing and note the possible transferability of this technique to other diverse contexts.

The Norwegian context

Norway's population is five million (Statistics Norway, 2014). Around 500,000 people are immigrants, and 100,000 are the children of immigrants, around 12 per cent of the total population in all. Immigrants are represented in all Norwegian municipalities, but Oslo has the largest proportion of its population non-native, with 28 per cent foreign-born. The largest groups are from Poland, Sweden, Lithuania, Germany and Denmark. The number of immigrants residing in Norway varies according to the government's immigration policy, labour market needs and shifting global crises.

In the school year 2012/13, approximately 7 per cent of all students in compulsory school received special language training. Of these, 60 per cent were given bilingual subject teaching, 15 per cent mother-tongue teaching, and 15 per cent both. In terms of adaptive education for these more recent minorities, mother-tongue teaching and bilingual pedagogy have been a matter of much debate, and there have been many policy changes in this area in recent decades. The Norwegian discourse has often related the use of mother tongue to learning and students' school results. Students from recent immigrant groups appear to achieve poorer school results than their majority peers (see for example Bakken, 2007; Roe and Hvistendahl, 2006).

During the 1980s the aim of education for newer minority students was functional bilingualism. This resulted in a high demand for qualified mother-tongue teachers. In 1997, however, this aim was abandoned, and since then Norway has had a transitional policy by which emergent bilingual students only have the right to teaching in basic Norwegian, and when necessary, also to mother-tongue teaching, bilingual subject teaching or both, until they are able to follow mainstream teaching. In effect, this also means that mother-tongue and bilingual subject teaching are subordinate to teaching in basic Norwegian. It is against this political climate that bilingual teachers' collaboration with other teachers needs to be understood.

In official documents, bilingual teachers are defined as teachers with an immigrant background (Norwegian Ministry of Education and Research, 2007). Traditionally, these teachers have supported emergent bilingual students during this transition phase, and very few of them have responsibilities in the mainstream. As a group, they make up only a small percentage of the total teaching force in Norway, and several researchers have drawn attention to their low status in the educational system (for example Engen and Ryen, 2009; Martincic, 2009; Myklebust, 1993; Valenta, 2009). Kjeldstadli links their low status to their travelling: 'Mother-tongue teachers in the school do not hold the same status, and are seldom employed at just one school and therefore, not able to make their mark on the institution' (2008: 119).

The study

The main objective of my doctoral study was to contribute to a better understanding of educational challenges and possibilities related to bilingual teachers' collaboration with other teachers in the education of emergent bilingual students in Norwegian compulsory schools. It was designed as a qualitative case study. The selection of two cases was a purposeful process, as I aimed to find information-rich cases that would shed light on my research question. At the same time these cases would ensure variety with respect to school level and location, the gender and language background of the teacher and the background of the students they taught. The first case is the study of Mohammed at Ullstad (conducted in autumn 2009), and this is the focus of this chapter. I did eleven days of fieldwork during a four-month period, made field notes, transcriptions, and when necessary, translated a selection of the audio recordings.

At the time of the study, Mohammed was around 40 years of age. He had moved from Somalia to Norway fifteen years earlier, thus being amongst the first Somali asylum seekers to come to the country. Mohammed had a good command of the Norwegian language, was knowledgeable about Norwegian society in general and the school system in particular, and was about to finish a subject teacher training programme for bilinguals, specializing in Somali and social sciences. In the school year 2009/10, Mohammed taught at three different schools. Ullstad was his main school, where he had a temporary 50 per cent position.

Ullstad is a lower secondary school located in a medium sized town in an urban area in East Norway. Fifteen per cent of the school's students speak languages other than Norwegian at home. At this school, Mohammed was responsible for the teaching of all emergent bilingual students from a Somali background. Many had no or little prior schooling, and some of them had received their first schooling in Arabic or Swahili while in transit. They had been in Norway between eight months and five years. Because of his job and his relatively long experience of living in Norway, Mohammed also had a lot of contact after school hours with his students' parents and with other Somali refugees who had arrived more recently.

From staging formal meetings to shadowing across the school

Before I became a teacher trainer and a researcher, I worked as a basic Norwegian teacher in a reception class for newly arrived students, so the work of teaching emergent bilingual students was not entirely new to me. It was, however, new from the viewpoint of the bilingual teacher. Therefore, I conducted a pre-study (September–October 2008), which proved to be decisive in the choice of method for the main study. On the basis of some of the literature I had read on bilingual teachers' collaboration with other teachers (for example Hauge, 2007; Myklebust, 1993; Vedøy, 2008), I found myself preoccupied with formal teacher meetings, especially from a conversation analytical point of view, influenced by Linell (1998, 2009; Linell and Gustavsson, 1987). Norwegian literature on bilingual teachers points to the lack of formal meeting places, and reminds us of their importance not only for the quality of the teaching but also as a means to create a space for the bilingual teacher. Hauge, for example, argues that the centrality of bilingual teachers in the school's planning activities may be seen as an index of the extent to which the school views diversity as an asset or as a problem.

Because I was unable to find a bilingual teacher who participated in this type of meeting on a regular basis, I arranged four meetings between a bilingual teacher from a Polish language background and a natural science teacher (Dewilde, 2009). I was inspired by Arkoudis (2005, 2006) who staged meetings between an ESL (English as a Second Language) and a natural science teacher in order to explore how they constructed their professional relationship and negotiated their subject knowledge when planning a science lesson together. In addition to observing and audio recording these meetings, I observed their joint science lessons and interviewed each teacher individually.

Early in my pre-study, it became apparent that collaboration between the two teachers was by no means limited to the meeting room. They conversed continually while moving between the team room, their desks and the classroom. Walking with them allowed me to ask questions and gave me deeper insight into their teaching of a newly arrived student. I made two main decisions with regard to methodology. I found that simply recording the teachers' conversations during formal meetings would not provide enough insights into teacher collaboration. Influenced by Creese's (2005) study on (bilingual) EAL (English as an Additional Language) teachers in three London schools, I decided to combine recording with fieldwork as this would enable me to study naturally-occurring teacher collaboration in different settings. Not limited to meeting rooms, team rooms and classrooms, I opted for a shadowing technique in order to have frequent field conversations with my key participants while on the move. My curiosity about the bilingual teacher's conversations with her student in Polish, led me to realize the importance of multilingual data in my study, as part of information-rich case studies. A discursive shadowing technique meant a more open and explorative approach to teacher collaboration. Instead of viewing collaboration predominantly as interaction during planned meetings, I now searched for collaboration in all possible forms, that is, not only through verbal interaction but also in more indirect ways, such as when the bilingual teachers collected periodic plans containing an overview of all teaching and homework during a set period.

Shadowing as a qualitative research strategy

Across the social sciences, existing interpretive methods have been criticized as dealing poorly with movement, multiplicity and change. Law and Urry (2004) argue that instead of wanting to pin down and dissect these phenomena, researchers should try to engage with the fleeting – that which slips and slides between one place and another – and the multiple. Büscher *et al.* claim that when researchers immerse themselves in the mobile world of their study objects, they are able to understand movement not only as regulated by systems, but also as methodically generative (2011: 7).

Shadowing is an example of such a mobile method, as it involves 'following selected people in their everyday occupations for a time' (Czarniawska, 2007: 17). McDonald shows that in social sciences the purposes for a shadowing technique may differ according to the purpose of the study (2005: 461). Shadowing is used for experiential learning such as in vocational education, in studies that aim to record behaviour, and in studies that aim to understand participants' perspectives.

A characteristic of shadowing is what McDonald calls the 'running commentary' from the person being shadowed in response to the researcher's questions (2005: 456). The adjective 'running' is well suited to the movement, but I prefer 'dialogue' to 'commentary' because it underlines the reflexive potential of shadowing. Jirón also sees shadowing as a reflexive practice (2011: 36–7). She argues that 'becoming the shadow' is a reflexive endeavour, involving not only the acknowledgment of routines, 'but also entering into practices, into dialogue and interaction in a constant engagement with the people whose lives they constitute'. Here, Jirón understands interaction as dialogue, as well as embodied interaction. She concludes that the researcher's position and the method used always need to be adapted reflexively.

Both Jirón (2011) and McDonald (2005) note the considerable amount of material produced by shadowing. In fact, McDonald uses this as a reason for advising the shadowing researcher against audio recording. I too have chosen to audio record conversations between my key participants and myself, and between my key participants and their colleagues. This made the selection for analysis more complex. However, it also provided increased opportunities for reflexive research. This extra layer is at the core of discursive shadowing (Dewilde and Creese, forthcoming). In addition, in a study of bilingual education where part of the key participants' interaction is in languages the researcher does not understand, audio recordings are essential for gaining access to these conversations.

The conversations between my key participant and myself do not only become a means of discussing unfolding and exploratory thoughts and preliminary analyses; they also become a source of additional interactional field material in which I participate. Treating the shadowing conversations as conversational events and making them available as data, the researcher's voice is worked into the analysis, playing a part in shaping and representing the social action that is observed. This requires the researcher to pay attention to her own voice, taking responsibility for what she says, how she says it, and to whom (Heller, 2008: 251). This raises issues of boundaries and ethics while on the move that call for 'a research ethics on the move' (Dewilde, 2013: 72–6).

In sum, discursive shadowing involves the study of individuals over a period of time. The joint movement, common reflection and ubiquitous recordings create opportunities to understand the key participant's everyday life. In the next two sections, I explore and illustrate these points further.

Negotiating access and building relationships and loyalty

Shadowing is a technique that requires constant closeness, perhaps closer than most other qualitative research methods, in terms of both physical and social proximity. While it potentially provides the researcher with rich data about the research participants and about the landscape they move in, this intimacy also contributes to the complex dynamics between the researcher and the participant. Jirón reminds us that the researcher's position and methods constantly need to be adapted reflexively (2011: 37). I exemplify this complex relationship building by illustrating how it might lead to negotiation of access to certain places and to feelings of loyalty towards the key participants.

Returning to the case at hand, towards the end of the fieldwork Mohammed discovered that only one of his four students had come to the laboratory in the school's basement for the upcoming science lesson. He told me he would go and look for the other three, who might be hiding in the school's reception class on the second floor. I would have liked to have joined him in his quest to find the students, but felt unable to negotiate this with him. My field notes record:

> I would have liked to join Mohammed find the students who skipped class, but he didn't invite me. I don't feel as if I am in any position to ask him if I can join him either. Maybe he wants to save me the trip up and down. He may not think it is relevant for me to join him either. After all, I told him that I am here to study his collaboration with other teachers.[3]

There are many possible reasons why Mohammed chose to leave me when he went searching for the students who were skipping classes: he may have found it embarrassing that he had to do so often, sometimes even losing them on the way to the classroom. He may have wanted to spare me the long walk between floors, or he may not have understood my rationale for wanting to accompany him, as no 'real teaching' was going on. Either way, discursive shadowing enabled me to grasp the centrality of this particular kind of movement in Mohammed's work, which is again interesting, given the lack of conversation between Mohammed and his colleagues concerning the students' possible reasons for skipping classes.

The field notes reveal my frustration at the failure to shadow Mohammed as he travelled upstairs, but they also reminded me of the significance of the missed event and the recurring matter of students avoiding lessons. Having been left behind deprived me of the possibility of reflecting with Mohammed on what was happening. Instead, I had to listen to the recording when I was back at the office after my day in the field, and wait for the arrival of the translated transcriptions of the talks in Somali with the students. At the same time, this event is also a reminder of Mohammed's power as an informant, and how he left me with little agency.

The physical and social proximity of shadowing may lead to feelings of loyalty or, conversely, a lack of loyalty. In Mohammed and Sverre's joint natural science lesson, Mohammed had agreed beforehand that after the first half hour of teaching he would take his students to the library to do exercises while the rest of the class had a test. When Mohammed got up and informed me that he was taking the two students to the library, I was taken by surprise and needed to gather my belongings. When I was ready to leave, Sverre accompanied me to the door and started discussing Mohammed's situation. My field notes record:

> Sverre comes with me to the door and tells me that it must be difficult to be a teacher aid when he (Mohammed) has to chase students who skip classes all the time. He tells me that I probably see more than he does, and he wonders if the students skip other classes besides science classes. I answer that it does not look like they skip class when they are in the reception class, but that they do so in other classes. I felt uncomfortable answering this question because I got this information by shadowing Mohammed. In a way, I felt as if I was betraying Mohammed.

These field notes record a different set of affordances gained from not shadowing Mohammed. Staying behind allowed Sverre's voice to be heard. Here, Sverre positions me as somebody who has information he was curious about, but cannot access. However, the field notes also reveal ethical concerns. I felt uncomfortable conversing about Mohammed and his students with another teacher, and being asked to share information or insights gained through shadowing. During my fieldwork I had both observed and talked with Mohammed about the students' lack of understanding of the subject content but as Mohammed did not talk about this with other teachers, I felt I couldn't do so either. The constant companionship that Mohammed and I had established created feelings of loyalty and alignment that shaped the way I considered ethical issues in the field.

Access to unexpected people and interactions

Quinlan (2008) and Gilliat-Ray (2011) have pointed to the opportunities shadowing researchers have for gaining access to unexpected places and situations. I too experienced an unexpected situation when shadowing

Mohammed, in which unforeseen people talked about unanticipated topics. During a two-hour parent–teacher meeting I observed Mohammed mediating between two members of staff (the assistant principal and the teacher responsible for the reception class) and six Somalian parents. During my fieldwork, I had become aware of the centrality of Mohammed's work with his students' parents, as he often chose to phone them or was asked to do so by other teachers. However, this meeting provided me with new insights into the complexities of teacher collaboration as well as bringing ethical challenges.

Prior to my study, the parents had been informed about the project and had signed a letter of consent on behalf of their children. Before the meeting started, they were reminded of the study and asked by the bilingual teacher if it was acceptable for me to observe and record their participation at the parent–teacher meeting. All consented. However, I became uncertain about the formalities and I phoned Norwegian Social Science Data Services, who had formally approved my study. The caseworker told me that as long as I anonymized the parents and had their oral consent on tape, there should be no problem. One of Mohammed's tasks at the meeting was translating between the parents and the staff. The atmosphere seemed relaxed and all parties talked and laughed. After the meeting the staff and Mohammed expressed contentment and did not discuss the meeting any further.

However, when working through the transcripts and translations, I was troubled to find large amounts of private talk by the parents about their children, their challenging housing conditions, and their dissatisfaction with the school. It became apparent that Mohammed had chosen not to translate this to the staff, even though the parents had intended him to do so. There are possibly various reasons for this, including Mohammed's wish to protect the parents or, perhaps, the Norwegian staff. At one point, Mohammed even reminded the parents about the audio recorder. He may have thought that exposing the parents' and students' private situation could be detrimental to them as members of a minority group in Norway.

When I asked Mohammed about this in a semi-structured interview about a year after the fieldwork, he promptly replied that he would have preferred it if there had been an external translator who did not know the parents. This would have allowed him to focus on being a bilingual teacher. The reason he gave for not translating private issues and the parents' discontentment with the school was that he wanted to be able to face the staff, the parents and the students.

In dealing with this ethical event in my analysis, I tried to adhere to my research question about teacher collaboration and be sensitive to the information that would answer it, without intruding on the parents' privacy.

My focus on these ethical issues is in line with Stake's advice not to probe into sensitive issues that have low-priority for the researcher in qualitative case studies (2008: 205). In my analysis I wrote about Mohammed's challenge of combining the roles of bilingual teacher and translator but wrote less about the parents' more private challenges, since these were not the focus of my study.

How did discursive shadowing afford insight into the complexities of teacher collaboration with regard to Mohammed's mediator role between school and home? First of all, the translations and transcriptions of the parents' and Mohammed's talk reminded me of the shortcomings of the school's understandings in meetings of this kind. Things are not always what they appear to be. Secondly, it made me recognize Mohammed's power, as well as his loneliness as he tried to combine his roles as translator and bilingual teacher. These are important issues but he never discussed them with his colleagues during my fieldwork, and I never thought of asking him about them when he made frequent phone calls to the students' homes.

Discursive shadowing created valuable opportunities for accessing unexpected people and topics of interaction. It highlighted ethical issues when parents raised their concerns but Mohammed's translations of these meetings were not what I anticipated. The combination of discursive shadowing with semi-structured interviews enabled me to ask Mohammed about unresolved issues.

Conclusion

As I stated at the outset of this chapter, bilingual teachers' status in the Norwegian school system is low (Engen and Ryen, 2009; Martincic, 2009; Myklebust, 1993; Valenta, 2009), and they are an under-researched group. It felt like it was my responsibility to find a methodology that would produce rich material and give an illuminating, complex and multifaceted account of the bilingual teachers' work. I became aware of the importance of moving with the bilingual teachers and reflecting upon their work by means of running conversations, which I recorded while they were on the move. The discursive shadowing technique perfectly suited the study, their work and their collaboration with others.

Moving around the school with them, instead of trying to pin down collaboration through the formal meetings and joint lessons, made me understand the complexity of their work in several ways (Büscher et al., 2011). The embodied interaction (Jirón, 2011) of walking with Mohammed allowed me to acknowledge his routines, and thus get closer to the experience of bilingual teachers and their collaboration with others. It gave insights into the challenges this movement could cause when Mohammed left me behind while searching for students who were skipping classes. At the same time, his going off alone illustrates that the proposed mobile method of discursive shadowing is constantly negotiated with the bilingual teacher, with concomitant shifts in the balance of power.

Secondly, the fact that shadowing gives the researcher access to unexpected people and interaction allows flexibility and new possibilities of exploring the multiplicity of bilingual teachers' work and collaboration. Mohammed's role in the parent–teacher meeting yielded invaluable information about bilingual teachers as mediators between school and families. However, access to new people and conversations raises issues of boundaries and ethics. In the case of the parent–teacher meetings, the ethical moment was postponed until I had the translated transcripts. The fact that Somali parents may be seen as a vulnerable group in Norwegian society adds further complication (Holm, 2011).

Is discursive shadowing in linguistically diverse schools transferable to other diverse contexts or to other aspects of diversity? As I have said, I do not believe that discursive shadowing is necessarily the best method for studying diversity, but it may well provide different insights. It lends itself to the study of individuals whose working lives are characterized by movement, be it a multilingual taxi driver in a metropolitan city, a cycling tourist guide, a cleaner from a minority background, a commuter living in the countryside and working in the city, or a wheelchair user. Moving and reflecting together are likely to provide new knowledge related to different types of diversity, and yield complex accounts of individuals. In all cases, relationship building, negotiation of access and ethical concerns while on the move are essential.

References

Arkoudis, S. (2005) 'Fusing pedagogic horizons: Language and content teaching in the mainstream'. *Linguistics and Education*, 16 (2), 173–87.

— (2006) 'Negotiating the rough ground between ESL and mainstream teachers'. *The International Journal of Bilingual Education and Bilingualism*, 9 (4), 415–33.

Bakken, A. (2007) *Virkninger av tilpasset språkopplæring for minoritetsspråklige elever: En kunnskapsoversikt* [Effects of adapted education for minority language students]. NOVA Report, 10 (7). Oslo: Norsk institutt for forskning om oppvekst, velferd og aldring.

Büscher, M., Urry, J. and Witchger, K. (2011) 'Introduction: Mobile methods'. In Büscher, M., Urry, J., and Witchger, K. (eds) *Mobile Methods*. London: Routledge, 1–19.

Creese, A. (2005) *Teacher Collaboration and Talk in Multilingual Classrooms*. Clevedon: Multilingual Matters.

Czarniawska, B. (2007) *Shadowing and Other Techniques for Doing Fieldwork in Modern Societies*. Malmö: Liber.

Denzin, N.K. and Lincoln, Y.S. (2011) 'Introduction: The discipline and practice of qualitative research'. In Denzin, N.K. and Lincoln, Y.S. (eds), *The Sage Handbook of Qualitative Research*. 4th ed. Thousand Oaks, CA: Sage, 1–20.

Dewilde J. (2009) 'Teacher collaboration: A study of topics in planning sessions between a science and a bilingual teacher'. In Kjørven, O.K. and Ringen, B.-K. (eds), *Teacher Diversity in Diverse Schools: Challenges and opportunities for teacher education*, Vallset: Oplandske.

— (2013) 'Ambulating Teachers: A case study of bilingual teachers and teacher collaboration'. Ph.D. diss., University of Oslo.

Dewilde, J. and Creese, A. (forthcoming) *Shadowing in Linguistic Ethnography: Situated practices and circulating discourses in multilingual schools*.

Engen, T.O. and Ryen, E. (2009) 'Lærermangfold og flerkulturell opplæring. Tospråklige lærere i norsk skole' [Teacher diversity and multicultural education. Bilingual teachers in Norwegian schools]. *NOA: norsk som andrespråk*, 2, 41–57.

Gilliat-Ray, S. (2011) '"Being there": The experience of shadowing a British Muslim hospital chaplain'. *Qualitative Research*, 11 (5), 469–86.

Hauge, A.-M. (2007) *Den felleskulturelle skolen*. Oslo: Universitetsforlaget.

Heller, M. (2008) 'Doing ethnography'. In Wei, L. and Moyer, M.G. (eds), *The Blackwell Guide to Research Methods in Bilingualism and Multilingualism*. Malden, MA: Blackwell, 249–62.

Holm, I.M. (2011) 'Somaliere og norsk skole: En studie av somaliere i Norge med særlig fokus på relasjoner mellom lærere og foreldre' [Somalis and Norwegian schools: A study of Somalis in Norway with a particular focus on the relations between teachers and parents]. Ph.D. diss., University of Tromsø.

Jirón, P. (2011) 'On becoming "la sombra/the shadow"'. In Büscher, M., Urry, J. and Witchger, K. (eds) *Mobile Methods*. London: Routledge, 36–53.

Kjeldstadli, K. (2008) *Sammensatte samfunn: Innvandring og inkludering* [Complex societies: Immigration and inclusion]. Oslo: Pax.

Law, J. and Urry, J. (2004) 'Enacting the social'. *Economy and Society*, 33 (3), 390–410.

Linell, P. (1998) *Approaching Dialogue: Talk, interaction and contexts in dialogical perspective*. Amsterdam: John Benjamins.

— (2009) *Rethinking Language, Mind, and World Dialogically: Interactional and contextual theories of human sense-making*. Charlotte, NC: Information Age.

Linell, P. and Gustavsson, L. (1987) *Initiativ och respons om dialogens dynamik, dominans och koherens* [Initiative and response on the dynamics of dialogue, dominance and coherence]. Linköping: University of Linköping.

Martincic, J. (2009) 'Tospråklig opplæring i grunnskolen'. In Hvistendahl, R. (ed.), *Flerspråklighet i skolen*. Oslo: Universitetsforlaget, 95–105.

McDonald, S. (2005) 'Studying actions in context: A qualitative shadowing method for organizational research'. *Qualitative Research*, 5 (4), 455–73.

Myklebust, R. (1993) 'Undervisning på to språk: En analyse av den tokulturelle klassemodellen i Oslo: med vekt på den tospråklige undervisningen i matematikk og O-fag' [Teaching in two languages: An analysis of the bicultural class model in Oslo: with an emphasis on the bilingual teaching of mathematics and orienteering subject]. *NOA: norsk som andrespråk*, 17.

Norwegian Ministry of Education and Research (2007) *Equal Education in Practice! Strategy for better teaching and greater participation of linguistic minorities in kindergartens, schools and education 2007–2009*. Oslo: Ministry of Education and Research. Online. http://tinyurl.com/kbglffx (accessed May 2014).

Quinlan, E. (2008) 'Conspicious invisibility: Shadowing as a data collection strategy'. *Qualitative Inquiry*, 18 (8), 1480–99.

Roe, A. and Hvistendahl, R. (2006) 'Nordic minority students' literacy achievement and home background'. In Mejding, J. and Roe, A. (eds), *Northern Lights on PISA 2003: A reflection from the Nordic countries*. Copenhagen: Nordic Council of Ministers, 113–27. Online. http://tinyurl.com/qbb6wa2 (accessed May 2014).

Stake, R.E. (2008) 'Qualitative case studies'. In Denzin, N.K. and Lincoln, Y.S. (eds) *Strategies of Qualitative Inquiry*. Los Angeles: Sage, 119–49.

Statistics Norway (2014) 'Population'. Online. www.ssb.no/en/befolkning (accessed May 2014).

Valenta, M. (2009) '"Who wants to be a travelling teacher?" Bilingual teachers and weak forms of bilingual education: The Norwegian experience'. *European Journal of Teacher Education*, 32 (1), 21–33.

Vedøy, G. (2008) 'En elev er en elev', 'barn er barn' og 'folk er folk': Ledelse i flerkulturelle skoler ['A student is a student', 'children are children', 'people are people': Leadership in multicultural schools]. Ph.D. diss., University of Oslo.

Endnotes

[1] The names of the schools, teachers and students have been changed. In Norway, students are on a first-name basis with their teachers at all levels of state education, since formal address in schools is anathema in Norwegian culture.

[2] It is common for Norwegian schools to organize their teachers in teacher teams, according to the grade they have the most responsibilities for, rather than according to the subjects they teach. Each team often has a common working area, called a 'team room'.

[3] While shadowing, I wore a shoulder bag carrying a small portable computer for making field notes. While the bilingual teachers were teaching, I would continuously note down my observations and reflections, and enrich them after the working day. All notes were taken in Norwegian, which was the natural thing to do since I was surrounded by Norwegian in the schools, and it was the common language between the participants and myself. I have translated the notes included in this chapter from Norwegian into English. I used the field notes for two purposes: to acquire ideas and insights from the social life that I observed during my fieldwork, and to make selections from the mass of audio recordings obtained during the fieldwork.

Chapter 2
Power and knowledge in research with immigrant teachers: Questioning the insider/outsider dichotomy
Clea Schmidt

Introduction
Research investigating diverse teacher and learner populations continues to gain momentum as school systems across the world attempt to educate ever larger numbers of students of different abilities and from a vast range of cultural, linguistic, ethnic, religious and socio-economic backgrounds. Manitoba, Canada is one such context where diversity, especially the cultural and linguistic diversity present among immigrant populations, is having a profound impact on the policies and practices of public education. Between 1997 and 2012, due to an aggressive immigration programme designed to attract skilled labour to the province, thousands of students and hundreds of teachers from various ethnicities, cultures, and language backgrounds other than English joined what had previously been relatively homogenous school populations.[1]

At the peak of this programme, the Provincial Nominee Program (PNP), over 11,000 newcomers and 200 internationally educated teachers arrived each year in Manitoba, which had an overall provincial population of 1.2 million (Schmidt et al., 2010). In response, the provincial government increased financial support for programming for English as an additional language (EAL) learners and for students from refugee and war backgrounds; produced its first ever EAL curriculum; developed an Action Plan for Ethnocultural Equity that emphasized anti-racist education and more equitable opportunities for students and teachers of non-white, non-English speaking backgrounds; and funded bridge programming for immigrant teachers who had been educated in other parts of the world and who wished to resume their careers in Manitoba.

Within the scope of research investigating the impact of diversity in schools, studies conducted with immigrant teachers have been gaining momentum. The Canadian research in this area tends to be premised on the understanding that the teaching force needs to reflect the diversity of student populations for newcomer receiving countries better to promote inclusion and affirmation of multilingualism and multiculturalism effectively (Ryan et al., 2009). Immigrant teachers, defined in this instance as teachers with internationally obtained teaching credentials and/or experience, as well as first generation newcomers who completed their teacher education in Canada, are one such diverse group that continues to be under-represented in the Canadian teaching profession (Canadian Teachers' Federation, 2006).

Though longitudinal research is needed to gauge immigrant teachers' long-term impacts in classrooms, schools, and wider educational communities effectively, recent empirical studies have begun to document the numerous strengths and contributions some immigrant teachers offer diverse K–12 schools (e.g. Schmidt, 2010a). As illustrated by some of the cases that have been researched, these strengths can include multilingualism, intercultural awareness, first-hand knowledge of immigrant and/or refugee experiences, knowledge of and experience with different education systems, extensive teaching experience, and advanced degrees in content areas and/or education (Schmidt and Block, 2010). Despite these many strengths, immigrant teachers with potential and proven contributions to the education of youth in Canadian schools are marginalized by systemic barriers facing them as newcomers and as teachers who differ from the predominantly white, middle-class, English-speaking, Canadian-born teaching force (Schmidt, 2010a).

Methodology

This chapter analyses a critical participatory action research project conducted in 2009/10 with six immigrant teachers working in a variety of capacities in K–12 schools in Manitoba. At the time of the study, some participants were working as full-time teachers, some were working as substitute or term contract teachers, and some were working as educational assistants. This project aimed to include and voice the perspectives of representatives from each of these different groups, and adopted many of the features of co-operative inquiry described by Heron and Reason (2006), including involving participants in decision making and in co-constructing the research. The research investigated the teachers' lived experiences, roles and perceived impact in schools.

The current chapter focuses not on the research findings *per se*, but rather on insights gleaned from the process of conducting collaborative research with immigrant teachers. Data include reflections stemming from researcher fieldnotes and a journal kept for the duration of the study, as well as critical political discourse analysis (Fairclough and Fairclough, 2012) of guidelines provided for action researchers at the University of Manitoba (UM) (n.d.).

The chapter, framed within a critical theoretical lens, draws upon insights from the critical participatory action research project to analyse the relevance of this methodology for scholarship conducted with marginalized groups in education. Focusing on the central issue of researcher and participant positionality in the research process, notions of cultural 'insiders' and 'outsiders' are interrogated from a critical pedagogical stance that seeks to complicate and disrupt traditional understandings of expertise and ownership of knowledge (Kincheloe, 2008). In the process of exploring critical participatory action research and questioning traditional assumptions about the ownership and conduct of research, this chapter offers a response to UM's restrictive guidelines for conducting action or practitioner research. The chapter concludes with recommendations for informing educational research with diverse populations.

Critical participatory action research with immigrant teachers

Critical participatory action research has the potential to help redress the imbalance in educational research that tends to marginalize, and in many instances exclude altogether, the voices and concerns of immigrant teachers. As Gaventa and Cornwall elaborate:

> Participatory research has long held within it implicit notions of the relationships between power and knowledge. Advocates of participatory action research have focused their critique of conventional research strategies on structural relationships of power and the ways through which they are maintained by monopolies of knowledge, arguing that participatory knowledge strategies can challenge deep-rooted power inequities.
> (Gaventa and Cornwall, 2001: 71)

Immigrant teachers have been identified as a marginalized group in Canadian education worthy of research focus because the overall teacher surplus in Canada means immigrant teachers tend to be less of a priority in immigration and labour market policy and funding agendas. They frequently face employment discrimination in the education system despite being certified in Canada, and regardless of whether they have superior qualifications to Canadian-born and educated teachers or relevant experience in Canadian schools (Schmidt 2010a).

Immigrant teachers

According to Kincheloe, opening the research agenda to be more inclusive of marginalized voices is essential for legitimizing traditionally devalued forms of knowledge:

> A critical complex epistemology is dedicated to bringing individuals who have been traditionally excluded to the scholarly conversation no matter how déclassé such an objective appears to the privileged epistemological trolls.
>
> (Kincheloe, 2008: 58)

In the critical participatory action research study conducted with immigrant teachers, bringing the teachers to the scholarly conversation meant actively engaging them in designing, co-constructing, and carrying out the research. The teachers themselves selected focus group discussions as their preferred method of collecting data, and determined the number, timing, locations, and themes of the focus group meetings. For the focus group meetings, a school all of the participating teachers were familiar with in a personal or professional capacity was chosen as the site. Virtually all the participating teachers had spent time in the school in one form or another, as a volunteer, as a substitute teacher, as an educational assistant, as a full-time teacher, and/or as a parent. The school administrator at the time of the study was an immigrant teacher herself and extremely supportive of hiring immigrant teachers and foregrounding issues affecting their ability to access the school system in Manitoba. A socio-economically, culturally, and linguistically diverse student and staff demographic in the school, coupled with a very active anti-racist agenda that manifested in extensive professional development for school staff and various integrated curricular and extra-curricular programming for students and parents, meant the environment was a supportive and inclusive one in which to meet. The teacher-researcher-participants[2] took turns chairing the discussions. They determined what kind of professional development they felt they would benefit from at the conclusion of the research, and identified a series of job search workshops that were then organized and delivered by the university researchers who were partnering the project.

On account of the established inequities facing immigrant teachers, and with the need to have a more collaborative conversation than more traditional forms of research allow, critical participatory action research was identified as the most promising research methodology to challenge conventional understandings of who owns and enacts the research agenda and whose knowledge is valid. As I elaborate elsewhere:

17

> The critical aspect of the methodology challenge[s] existing inequities that marginalize immigrant teachers in K–12 schools and works toward social change; the participatory dimension ensure[s] that the immigrant teachers have ownership of the research process; and the action research component facilitate[s] sustainable (i.e., ongoing) outcomes that will directly impact the teachers, their professional practices, and the schools and classrooms in which they work.
>
> (Schmidt, 2010b: 366)

Challenging traditional understandings of voice and ownership manifested in the critical participatory action research by the fact that the agenda was mutually determined, with the balance of power in decision-making resting with the teacher-researcher-participants. Ownership of the research products, too, were shared. All teacher-researcher-participants received copies of the full transcripts of focus group discussions and one used the issues and topics raised within the focus group discussions as a springboard for designing her Masters thesis on the topic of immigrant teacher integration. Here, then, research conducted in partnership between a white, Canadian-born university researcher and immigrant teachers of Indian and Filipino backgrounds informed future research that was led and carried out by one of the immigrant teachers independently. The collaborative research served in this instance as an opportunity for mentoring an immigrant teacher in the research process and scaffolding her subsequent research design and implementation.

While significant for advancing an overall equity agenda in educational policies, practices, and scholarship, research conducted with immigrant teachers is nevertheless fraught with complexity and raises concerns about issues of voice, ownership, and representation. In a discussion of researcher positioning and reflexivity in which Lee and Simon-Maeda compare and contrast the complexities that emerged in their respective studies of researching 'the other' and 'one's own kind', they warn that 'the white critical feminist's best intentions to avoid marginalizing women of color in her study may in fact reproduce the same oppressive conditions she claims to be concerned about' (2006: 575).

Yet Lee and Simon-Maeda also acknowledge in conducting research with minority groups that social divisions are complex, and that:

> we are all subjugated to greater or lesser degrees in various sectors of our lives; a state of affairs that oftentimes creates a fuzzy boundary between insider/outsider positionings and allows

(read: *behooves*) those in more advantageous positions to speak in solidarity with (and not on behalf of) oppressed minorities.

(Lee and Simon-Maeda, 2006: 576, italics original)

This point is significant in the light of Lee and Simon-Maeda's analysis of insider/outsider positioning primarily with respect to race. As I reflect on my researcher positioning in relation to the immigrant teachers who participated in the critical participatory action research project, insider and outsider dimensions proved to be dynamic, evolving, negotiated, and context-dependent, with no single position fixed throughout the course of the research or even indeed within a single focus group discussion. While I acknowledge the privileged position I occupied as a white, Canadian-born university-based researcher, many other complex facets of my identity intersected with the complex positions and identities of the teacher-researcher-participants. We differed in our positions in that I was Canadian-born and educated while the teachers were born and educated abroad, though some had also pursued university coursework in Canada for accreditation purposes. I was therefore perceived as someone who had experience and an unquestioned place within the Canadian education system. Though my position as a university educator and researcher was considered prestigious by some, others among the teacher-researcher-participants had occupied more advanced positions, for example as a Dean of Teacher Education, in their home countries.

Those of us involved in the study were all female, and I perceived a comfort, a rapport, and a banter that ensued in part because of that shared characteristic. I was older than some of the teacher-researcher-participants, but younger than others. One of the teachers who had more than thirty years' experience as an educator tended to be looked on among the entire group as an authority on educational practices given her demonstrated passion and enthusiasm for the career to which she had dedicated much of her life and her thoughtful reflection derived from the considerable hindsight of a lengthy period in various classrooms and schools. I was pregnant with my first child during the study and most in the group were already mothers; this dynamic prompted a lot of expert advice and support directed towards me, for example with respect to balancing career and family.

In summary, to label myself an 'outsider' and the teacher-researcher-participants 'insiders' would be simplistic and overlook the complex relationship dynamics that manifest within the scope of a critical participatory action research project where focus groups discussions are conducted regularly with the same group members over a period of time.

The reality is, the teacher-researcher-participants and I shifted in and out of various roles as the project unfolded, with each taking the lead on different topics in different ways according to our varied interests and expertise. The learning that ensued was jointly constructed and reciprocal, a feature of collaborative research that is worth bearing in mind when considering guidelines for action researchers such as those addressed in the next section.

Response to 'Practitioner-Research': Guidelines for researchers and research ethics boards at the University of Manitoba

> The implementation of Policy 1406 on The Ethics of Research Involving Human Subjects has exposed some challenges regarding the review of research protocols submitted by 'practitioner-researchers'. 'Practitioner-researchers' are those individuals – typically in professional faculties and disciplines such as Education, Nursing, Medicine, Clinical Psychology, and Social Work – who conduct research on or with individuals (some of whom may be minors) who are receiving care or instruction from the investigator in his/her capacity as a service provider or educator. Because the practitioner-researcher is playing a dual role, there is the potential that certain ethical principles may be compromised, and accordingly, the practitioner-researcher must be acutely sensitive to questions about the voluntariness of participation, the vulnerability of participants, the potential for a conflict of interest on the part of the researcher, and whether consent is fully informed.
>
> The purpose of this document is to provide some guidelines to researchers on the preparation of research protocols for ethics review. These guidelines identify areas of concern in the evaluation of protocols that employ participatory, action or 'practitioner-research' approaches.
>
> (University of Manitoba, n.d.: 1)

The guidelines reveal a number of *a priori* suggestions regarding the ethical conduct of research involving human participants, and superficially offer pointers for action researchers about how to conduct themselves ethically and what types of justification the ethics review boards at this university require in the ethics review protocol. A more detailed analysis, however, reveals a number of problematic dimensions to these guidelines stemming

from the fact that they specifically target scholars who enga[ge in]
research, and emphasize how researchers must avoid coercio[n so]
that 'subjects are truly free to participate' (ibid.: 3). As I wi[ll show,]
guidelines, far from merely pointing out helpful tips for actio[n researchers,]
instead legitimize a problematic orientation to research that serves to:

1. stigmatize action research
2. disempower those engaged in the action research process, including researchers; participants; and other researchers, practitioners, and policy makers who may look to the research to inform their own practices
3. place undue burdens on action researchers to justify their methods to ethics review boards which may be biased against collaborative, constructivist, and critical approaches to research.

} wow!

The first concern involves the means by which the guidelines single out action research protocols as a problem for ethics review boards at the University of Manitoba and the fact that the guidelines appear to make no distinction between perceived problems with action research ethics submission protocols and perceived problems with action research itself. Such blurring of boundaries in the guidelines is evident in statements such as 'researchers must consider the advantages and disadvantages of using a population with whom they have a prior (and ongoing) relationship, and especially where that relationship involves an unequal relationship' (ibid.: 4). While the ethics submission protocol at UM requires researchers to explain how participants will be identified and recruited, the protocol does not explicitly require any researchers to consider the advantages and disadvantages of drawing on a particular participant pool. Is this requirement – to debate the merits of engaging participants the researcher has a professional relationship with – an aspect of research design the Office of Research Services feels action researchers may overlook, and something extra they should address, presumably because of the enhanced possibility of coercion noted above? It seems highly unlikely action researchers have not carefully considered the merit of involving the participants in question, since action research is premised on the notion that practitioners and their wider professional communities have something valuable to learn by engaging in research with their students, patients or clients.

'Unequal' is not defined in the document. Does the term refer to status, income, position, or the contributions of both researcher and participant to the relationship? Unless participant and researcher are in identical personal and professional circumstances and each contributes in exactly the same

..nanner to the relationship, then it would appear that having an 'equal' relationship is impossible. These restrictive elements of the guidelines can serve to cast doubt on, and possibly discourage researchers from employing, what is after all a well-established and widely used methodology that yields important insights not gleaned by other types of qualitative research.

Second, the guidelines are premised on the assumption that action researchers may be more likely than other types of researchers to engage in unethical practices and to coerce participants, when in fact proponents of action research are striving to validate previously marginalized voices and to conduct research *with* rather than *on* participants. The very use of the terms 'subject' and 'the researched' in the guidelines (ibid.: 2, 3) conveys a deficit orientation towards participants and suggests that these individuals altogether lack power, agency, and the ability to contribute to the research process as anything more than mere specimens to be observed and analysed. Such a view is aligned more with positivist and post-positivist paradigms, with their related set of ontological and epistemological assumptions, rather than with the participatory and critical paradigms embraced by proponents of action research. An equally problematic stance alongside portraying participants as specimens is to construe them as helpless victims of ruthless university researchers. While abuses in research have undoubtedly occurred, continue in some instances to happen, and should be guarded against (hence the Tri-Council Policy Statements as national guidelines for researchers across Canada), to suggest that participants altogether lack agency, or that roles of researcher and participants are static and one-dimensional demonstrates an ignorance of the complexity of relationships developed in the process of conducting action research and diminishes its contributions, since it is in these complex, reciprocal and dynamic relationships that rich and robust insights emerge.

Third, though the title of the document identifies researchers *and* research ethics boards as its intended audience, no suggestions whatsoever are provided for research ethics boards in evaluating action research protocols – a serious oversight considering it was the unspecified 'challenges regarding the review of research protocols submitted by "practitioner-researchers"' (ibid.: 1) that prompted the development of the guidelines in the first place. Providing imperatives to action researchers about what they should and must do to prove themselves ethical, while neglecting to provide any insight for reviewers of action research protocols or the chairs of ethics review boards, justifies potentially harsh evaluations of action research protocols. In the process, the subjective lenses and methodological biases of ethics review board members are ignored.

Critical educational theorists such as Kincheloe advocate m
the impact of validated knowledge or 'knowledge that is Formal, Int.
Decontextualized, Universalistic, Reductionistic, and One Dimer
(FIDUROD) (Kincheloe, 2008: 22), to create space for complex, rig
and transformative education. Yet as UM's guidelines demonstrate, despite
the potential, and indeed in many instances, demonstrated success of
participatory action research in challenging systemic inequities, conducting
studies informed by critical theory and newer qualitative paradigms is not
without its difficulties. It would seem that some Canadian researchers who
attempt to study various facets of diversity in education in partnership with
those most directly affected by policies and practices must in particular
settings contend with conservative research policies such as UM's guidelines
that cast doubt on the legitimacy of participatory forms of research.

Recommendations for researchers and research ethics boards

I would argue that the problem lies not so much in the tendency of action research to be potentially less voluntary, more coercive, and therefore more fraught with ethical concerns than other types of research involving human participants. Rather, the problem may well lie with the ethics boards themselves, which in some instances may be staffed by researchers who are proponents of FIDUROD and who actively seek to illegitimize participatory forms of research, the paradigms they are rooted in, and the new knowledges produced by these methodologies. However, as Kincheloe usefully reminds critical scholars, 'we cannot just wish that the producers of validated knowledge would simply change their epistemological ways and open new ways of thinking about how we see and report on the diverse phenomena surrounding us' (2008: 67).

Critical participatory action research shows great promise in opening up the epistemological spaces and scholarly conversations as encouraged by Kincheloe (2008), and though the challenges around voice, ownership and representation as articulated here and by Lee and Simon-Maeda (2006) may never be fully resolved, awareness of them and attempts to mitigate them can prove fruitful as they did in the study analysed in this chapter. To support scholars who engage in critical participatory forms of research, I would suggest that more supportive guidelines might integrate successful examples of how researchers address the issues in their work. Further, I would encourage research ethics boards to ensure that a variety of scholarly stances are represented among their members and that protocols be reviewed more appropriately by researchers who have some knowledge of and experience with the types of research under review. The discussion presented here is an attempt to begin to challenge the methodological discrimination that has the potential to flourish under such guidelines as those developed by UM and suggests that all individuals and groups implicated in the research process, including ethics reviewers, have a responsibility to consider their positioning, lest certain forms of research are unduly delegitimized.

References

Canadian Teachers' Federation (2006) *Review of the Employment Equity Act: Into the future*. May. Paper submitted to the Labour Program of Human Resources and Social Development Canada, Ottawa.

Fairclough, I. and Fairclough, N. (2012) *Political Discourse Analysis: A method for advanced students*. London and New York: Routledge.

Gaventa, J. and Cornwall, A. (2001) 'Power and knowledge'. In Reason, P. and Bradbury, H. (eds) *Handbook of Action Research*. London: Sage, 71–82.

Heron, J. and Reason, P. (2006) 'The practice of co-operative inquiry Research "with" rather than "on" people'. In Reason, P. and Bradbury, H. (eds) *Handbook of Action Research: Concise Paperback Edition*. London: Sage, 144–54.

Kincheloe, J.L. (2008) *Knowledge and Critical Pedagogy: An introduction*. New York: Springer.

Lee, E. and Simon-Maeda, A. (2006) 'Racialized research identities in ESL/EFL research'. *TESOL Quarterly* 40 (3), 573–94.

University of Manitoba (n.d.) '"Practitioner-Research": Guidelines for researchers and research ethics boards at the University of Manitoba'. Online. http://umanitoba.ca/research/orec/media/practitioner_research_guidelines.pdf (accessed 10 July 2014).

Ryan, J., Pollock, K. and Antonelli, F. (2009) 'Teacher diversity in Canada: Leaky pipelines, bottlenecks, and glass ceilings'. *Canadian Journal of Education*, 32 (3), 591–617.

Schmidt, C. (2010a) 'Systemic discrimination as a barrier for immigrant teachers'. *Diaspora, Indigenous, and Minority Education*, 4 (4), 235–52.

— (2010b) 'Towards equity for internationally educated teachers in teacher education field experiences'. In Falkenberg, T. and Smits, H. (eds), *Field Experiences in the Context of Reform of Canadian Teacher Education Programs*. Winnipeg, MB: University of Manitoba. Vol. 2, 359–68.

Schmidt, C. and Block, L. (2010) 'Without and within: The implications of employment and ethnocultural equity policies for internationally educated teachers'. *Canadian Journal of Educational Administration and Policy*, 100, 1–23.

Schmidt, C., Young, J. and Mandzuk, D. (2010) 'The integration of immigrant teachers in Manitoba, Canada: Critical issues and perspectives'. *Journal of International Migration and Integration*, 11 (4), 1–14.

Endnotes

[1] While Manitoba has always had a diverse student population with large numbers of First Nations, Métis, and Inuit students and a long history of immigration from Eastern Europe, large-scale immigration from other regions of the world was uncommon prior to the Provincial Nominee Program.

[2] The use of this term reflects the multiple roles played by each person involved in the research.

Chapter 3
Unsettling truths: Post-structural ethnography as a tool to trouble schooling exclusions
Kathryn Edgeworth

Introduction

How to conduct research into the lives of ethnically and culturally diverse 'others' in education in ways that empower the participants of the research and do no harm is a question that has troubled the minds of many researchers. Issues of power, of both the researcher and the researched, are ever present, and credibly representing the lives of marginalized groups in education in ways that trouble the exclusions they experience is an epistemological, theoretical and methodological challenge. Finding ways to engage with these concerns to create representations that open up the lives of marginalized 'others' in education to understanding and change is difficult research terrain.

In my ethnographic study of cultural diversity in rural schools in Australia, I spent one school year gathering data in order to examine the social and cultural principles that explained the lived experience of ethnic and religious minority young people in rural communities there. I began the process of data collection, intending to unpack the schooling scenes and narratives that presented at research sites and to move beyond mere representation to understand how power was configured in schools and its impact on the everyday lives of my ethnic and religious minority participants. I wanted to write a rich description of the lives of these students that critically illustrated how they were produced in everyday relations of power that are taken for granted. I sought to understand and write about how students were constructed within frameworks of understanding that limited who they were allowed to 'be' and how they were able to 'do' school. I did not seek to offer readers the truth about the lives of these students, but sought to offer a reading of their experiences that spoke against existing and prevailing ways of understanding schooling life and that revealed the tensions and possibilities of social space.

In terms of engaging with a historical record of practice, this was not a simple task. While there is a long tradition in education of research concerned with social justice, identity and schooling, there exists only a small body of work concerned with the methodological and philosophical considerations and implications of carrying out post-structural ethnographies of education and schooling (Britzman, 1995; Popoviciu et al., 2006; St Pierre and Pillow, 2000; Stronarch and MacLure, 1997). There is a limited number of works that adopt a post-structural ethnographic approach to researching ethnic and/or cultural difference in schools (see, for example, Keddie, 2011; Oikonomidoy, 2007; Rasmussen and Harwood, 2003; Youdell, 2006a, 2006b, 2011).

The purpose of this chapter is threefold. First, it illustrates the methodological features of post-structural ethnography; second, it shows the practices of methodology, data analysis and representation that characterize post-structural ethnographic work with ethnic and cultural minorities as described in the previous section; and third, it provides examples of ethnographic practice that unsettle dominant constructions of schooling and which are helpful to other post-structuralist researchers working with issues of cultural diversity.

Rethinking ethnography: The discursive priorities of post-structural ethnography

Post-structural ethnography as a methodology has been successfully taken up in educational research to understand the lived experience of students whose identities constitute them outside the hegemonic mainstream. Working within (and against) a tradition of school ethnographies that focus on identity, schooling exclusions and issues of social justice (Gilbert and Gilbert, 1998; Mac an Ghaill, 1988; Thomson, 2002; Willis, 1977), this methodology draws attention to the commonalities in the way students' identities are formed in educational institutions, and suggests the processes by which schooling inclusions and exclusions are made and unmade. Understanding the axes of identity by which exclusion is produced and the ways that 'the *identity* of the excluded group is fundamental to their exclusion' (Youdell, 2006a) is a crucial starting point in troubling educational exclusions. Further, understanding 'who' a student gets to 'be' in schooling contexts in order to be recognizable provides a means to understand how processes of marginalization commonly play out in schools, as well as how difference is negotiated in the everyday by ethnic and/or cultural minority students. Indeed, Popoviciu, Haywood and Mac an Ghaill have suggested that post-structural school ethnographies are rich in promise for research that seeks to work with subordinated groups: 'Opening up a social world and sensitizing the researcher to alternative experiences and understandings to those of the dominant institutional explanations of what is institutionally going on' (Popoviciu *et al.*, 2006: 401).

'Ethnography' is a disputed term and means different things to different people. Traditionally, educational ethnographers have sought to study things in their natural environment and to understand the interpretations that people bring to things (Denzin and Lincoln, 2000):

> Educational ethnography has been described as 'research on and in educational institutions based on participant observation and/ or permanent recordings of everyday life in naturally occurring settings' (Delamont and Atkinson, 1995: 15). Ethnographic study requires 'direct observation, it requires being immersed in the field situation' (Spindler, 1982: 154) with the researcher as a major instrument of research.
>
> (Gordon *et al.*, 2001: 188)

With the advent of post-structuralism within the field of education, a challenge exists to think differently about the real in ethnographic representation and to do ethnography differently (Britzman, 1995). What doing ethnography differently means in a methodological sense is challenging work for the post-structuralist. Stronach and MacLure, for example, have suggested that:

> making deconstruction *familiar* – which would be the usual aim of a methods textbook ... [is to] reduce it to the predictability of a technology or a useful set of analytic tools. We are more concerned in the potential of deconstruction to make educational research *unfamiliar*.
>
> (Stronach and MacLure, 1997: 3)

Such thinking is in keeping with a post-structural philosophy that eschews certainty; that understands its task as being to unsettle truth, including any certainty attached to methodology and findings that are themselves recognized as being contingent and discursive. Taking up this challenge, my overriding desire in this chapter is to put post-structuralism to work. In doing so, the methodological considerations and practices guiding my own ethnographic work can be identified and laid open to readers. Having said this, I enumerate below some of the elements of post-structural ethnography guiding my own work.

An uncertain methodology

1. Post-structural ethnographies are guided by an ontology that is wary of 'objective' claims to knowledge. In my own research, I utilize the post-structural theories of Michel Foucault (1998, 2000, 2002a, 2002b), Judith Butler (1997, 2004) and Michel de Certeau (1984) as an epistemological lens for making sense of social life.
2. Post-structural ethnographies aim to make transparent the ways truths are constituted through discourse (both in terms of what is studied and how it is studied).
3. Post-structural ethnography involves understanding data as 'partial, situated and interested knowledge' (Kenway *et al.*, 2006: 41).
4. Just as it is important to recognize the constructed nature of 'truth', so it is important to acknowledge the way discourses form the objects of which they speak, and have productive capacity (Butler, 1997). With this theory in mind, in a methodological sense it is important to understand the way I continue to reinvoke such terms and, in doing so, extend the discursive process of giving performative force to the injurious name (Youdell, 2006b).
5. A post-structural approach to observation entails recognizing that analysis is taking place from the researcher's first moments in the field, as choices are made regarding where to look and what/whom to look at (or ignore), and how to make sense of data in terms of subjectivities taken up (or not) and discursive frames employed (or eschewed) (Rhedding-Jones 1996; Youdell 2006a). The processes that see data selectively reproduced in the writing up of research are thus mediated by recognition of the researcher's own discursive capacities – 'the discourse that I see and name' (Youdell 2006b: 513). In this sense, in selecting data for representation, I offer and make choices about compelling moments from the field that represent how knowledges and subjects are constituted.
6. Post-structural ethnography involves ethnographic authority stemming not from an interpretation of events as provided by the participant or researcher, but through transparency in the research process, particularly as this relates to the subjectivities brought to the data collection, analysis and writing up by the researcher. Meaning-making in relation to these subjectivities needs always to remain open to questioning.
7. I align myself with the proposition of Merriam *et al.* that the complexities of identity (of both the researcher and researched) should

be taken up in the research process where there is recognition that during 'the course of a study, not only will the researcher experience moments of being both insider and outsider, but that these positions are relative to the cultural values and norms of both the researcher and the participants' (Merriam *et al.*, 2001: 415–16). Such an argument recognizes that the self is not unitary, and as such, there is a blurring of distinctions that can be made between insider and outsider boundaries (Subreenduth and Rhee, 2010). It recognizes the situated nature of identity, and calls for subjectivities to be made transparent through methodology in order to make recognizable how discourses render knowledges and performativities. This practice seems particularly important when researchers from the dominant cultural mainstream research ethnic and/or cultural 'others' within society.

8. 'Even in the most "empowering" research, issues of power are never absent' (Scott and Usher, 1999: 18). Thus, in writing the narrative of young, ethnic minority and religious 'others', I acknowledge the subjectivity of my position as a white, female researcher, and the cultural prism through which I make meaning and interpret events. In terms of the research represented in this chapter, my own experience of Australian rural life profoundly shapes my own subjectivity, as well as my own orientations to the research endeavour. Similarly, my location in rural spaces as a white, educated, English-speaking adult woman, shapes not only what is possible for me in personal terms, but also shapes how I am perceived and my relationships in research sites. These issues of power and positionality are explored in post-structural ethnographies through processes of reflexivity.

These conceptual tools provide a means in this chapter to think through regimes of marginalization and privilege in schools. In the following section, I go on to illustrate how this methodological framework is taken up in a post-structural ethnographic study of ethnic and religious minority students in rural Australia.

An example of a post-structural ethnographic study: Methodology in action

In 2006, I spent one full school year collecting data to understand the workings of power, privilege, whiteness and difference in the lives of six ethnic and religious minority students studying at three rural high schools in Australia. The high schools were located in towns with populations ranging from 2,700 to 30,000 people, each some four to five driving hours from a

Post-structural ethnography

capital city. Ethnic and religious minority students generally constituted less than 3 per cent of the total school population in each school. While only small numbers of immigrants and refugees have arrived to study in rural Australia, the confined nature and size of many Australian country towns means that they are often highly visible because of their ethnicity, religion and culture. Over the course of three school terms (a school term amounts to a period of approximately ten to 13 weeks), I observed ethnic and religious minority students as they went about their schooling lives. Observation involved sitting in on lessons with each participant on approximately twenty occasions, observing them in playgrounds, and following them (more or less discretely) as they went about their school day. What I tried to do was follow the students to observe how they did individually at school, all the while recording my observations of the discourses framing their being and belonging in a field notebook. Semi-structured interviews were also conducted to explore discourses and their effects as they emerged in participant narratives. In this chapter I draw on the narratives of two students from the aforementioned study to illustrate how post-structural ethnographic studies of schooling can offer insight into, and challenge, schooling exclusions.

I choose to represent data as a series of vignettes, characterizing a shift away from traditional academic modes of representation to new ways of engaging with data and disseminating research. This presentation style is in keeping with the conventions of similar studies in the sociology of education (Youdell, 2006b, 2011), as well as more general trends in the reporting of ethnographic data where theatrical scripting is adopted to engage with the complexities of post-structural research (Goldstein, 2008). The vignettes in this chapter are drawn from transcripts of interviews and from my fieldnotes. Pseudonyms are deployed throughout this chapter to refer to participants and places.

In the following vignette I explore the schooling experiences of Khatria – the only female student from Afghanistan at Gundah High School at the time of my research. In a speech given at a school awards ceremony celebrating Khatria's academic achievements since arriving in Australia as a refugee, I illustrate how Khatria is produced through normative discourses governing the terms of her recognition. I aim to demonstrate how ethnographic data can be taken up by ethnographers and read again in light of the theories of post-structuralism.

The transcript that follows is of a speech given at an awards ceremony at Gundah High School in 2006. Given by a member of the school's executive staff, the speech was presented to an audience of approximately 800 school staff, students and families attending the Presentation Day ceremony.

Presentation day at Gundah High School, Australia

> The Gundah Teachers' Association Award, is presented to the student who has shown commitment and success towards Year 10 studies. Khatria Nazari has shown commitment across many subjects and she has a very interesting story.
>
> Khatria has only lived in Australia for sixteen months. She was born in southern Afghanistan when the Taliban government was in power. As a female in this society she was not allowed to attend school. Her family fled the country when Khatria was ten years old and they moved to Pakistan. This was the first time that she attended school for only one hour per day at the American Language Center. When she was fifteen years old Khatria moved to Gundah and attended her first ever real school. In 2006 Khatria has successfully completed Year 10 and has achieved outstanding results. She has received a ranking of second in Advanced History and third in Visual Arts, and also received certificates for sustained commitment to learning for Advanced English, Advanced Geography and Advanced Science.
>
> Khatria is an example of what can be achieved by any student if they choose to take the opportunities available at this outstanding educational facility.
>
> Congratulations Khatria and her family. Please put your hands together for Khatria Nazari.
> (Transcript of speech provided by teacher at Gundah High School)

In the following analysis, I engage with the discourses and truths that produce Khatria as a particular sort of schooling subject. I do so in order to illustrate the potential of post-structural ethnographies to disrupt what has been represented in the above speech as Khatria's real experience of schooling. I offer an alternative reading – a counter narrative – of Khatria's everyday schooling experience. In this framing of ethnography, I move beyond understanding how others make sense of social life to focus instead on the discursive construction of the student-subject. Method, in this sense, can be understood to involve recording the discourses that create and frame students' experience of schooling, and examining these discourses through a post-structural lens to suggest who a student has to be in order to be recognizable in social terms. In terms of engaging with a post-structural methodology, I claim only to provide a partial account of the discourses that operate in the setting under discussion. Both intentionally and unintentionally, discourses will have escaped my attention as a researcher, and other discourses will also be in play that are omitted in my 'reading' of the narrative.

Performative subjects: Mapping the contours of recognition and belonging

Gillborn and Youdell have suggested that 'ideal' students are constituted by discourses of ability and conduct; that students are not just thought of and described (named) as ideal *students*, but are also created and produced as ideal *learners* (2000, 2004). In this sense, Youdell makes a distinction between students and learners. That is, between those students who merely attend school, and those who are provided with opportunities to engage actively in learning opportunities. In keeping with this idea, I argue that Khatria is rewarded, via the speech at Presentation Day, for being both a good student and an ideal learner and is performatively constituted at Presentation Day in this image. In Khatria's case, intellectual capacity, hard work and struggle are rewarded and highlighted in the Presentation Day speech.

In the narrative presented, however, a 'charity discourse' (Choules, 2006) is invoked that implies Khatria has been the lucky recipient of Australia's, and more particularly, Gundah's, humanitarian largesse. To this extent, Khatria's own efforts in achieving academic success are discounted, and institutional structures and arrangements are given credit for promoting Khatria's newfound good fortune. In the speech, Khatria is made intelligible and recognized (Butler, 1997) as one of *us* (embraced by the West), however such recognition inevitably depends upon Khatria renouncing her association with the 'evil Arabs' of her past to align herself with her Western saviours who determine the racialized terms of her recognition. On this basis, Khatria must acknowledge the role of her rescuers in her success, and pay (if only silent) homage to their argument that her homeland is the place of 'Arab' persons who would de-value her.

In making this claim, I take up Butler's argument on the treatment of 'Arab looking persons', and Muslims in particular, as potential terrorists in the post-September 11th world. As Butler writes of this phenomenon:

> We now see ... a heightened surveillance of Arab peoples and anyone who looks vaguely Arab in the dominant racial imaginary, anyone who looks like someone you once knew who was of Arab

> descent, or who you thought was ... Various terror alerts that go out over the media authorize and heighten racial hysteria in which fear is directed anywhere and nowhere, in which individuals are asked to be on guard but not told what to be on guard against, so everyone is free to imagine and identify the source of terror.
>
> (2004: 39)

Engaging with this debate, I use the term 'Arab' in this discussion to refer to both Arabs and persons who might be considered to be of 'Arab' appearance. In deploying this term, I critically engage with the way diverse populations of people in Australia are racialized under the umbrella term 'Arab' as a result of the conflation of Islamic religious identity and 'Middle Eastern appearance' with Arab identity. In the Australian context, this conflation frequently entails the grouping of Arabic-speaking persons and persons of Middle Eastern and North African heritage with persons from Central and South Asian countries such as Afghanistan and Pakistan. Despite the fact that these latter countries are not generally regarded as 'Arab', an association with Islam appears to conflate religious identity with an Arab cultural identity. I cautiously engage with this term here to make sense of power and knowledge arrangements while critically recognising that 'Arabs' (real and imagined) are not a homogeneous identity category and understanding that this conflation rests upon, and reinscribes, far-reaching stereotypes of 'Arab' persons.

Returning to my analysis of the presentation day speech, in de Certeau's terms, such a speech act is a 'culturally creative act' (1984: 123), where Gundah is constituted by language as a place of 'real schooling' and, by corollary, Khatria is discursively made real to her Western benefactors by her successful adoption of their terms of conduct and ability (Gillborn and Youdell, 2000). Limited terms of belonging are thus on offer to Khatria, who seemingly must continue to display the attributes of the good student and ideal learner in order to continue to enjoy social recognition.

Thinking methodologically, it should be noted that this analysis is not neutral – it both describes the terms of Khatria's (mis)recognition and extends it. Taking up Butler's (1997) work on performativity, namely her consideration of the powers of language to name and wound, I point to the productive power of my own analysis to injure. For example, in naming Khatria as a refugee, I reinvoke a term with historicity; a term with an attachment to discourses of war, politics, poverty, need and globalization. In reproducing this term in my analysis, I recognize that discourses have both foreseen and unforeseen meaning attached to them, and that in their

Post-structural ethnography

iteration, I am 'implicated in ongoing processes of subjectivation' (Youdell, 2006a: 64).

On 'truth': Or how students are produced as subjects of normative discourse

Khatria is not alone in being represented as 'ideal' in the speech presented. The Australian education system, and Gundah High School in particular, are also discursively cast as ideal and as the educational saviour of Khatria – the 'in need' Afghan refugee. Prior to arriving at Gundah High School, the narrator suggests Khatria did not have access to a 'real school', so that in less than 18 months Gundah High has taken Khatria from a position of no formal schooling to educational success. It is the West that is credited with this result (with Gundah High School at the forefront of the campaign), having saved Khatria from the supposedly backward, unenlightened 'Arab' society from which she came that did not see fit to educate girls. Even in the country of safety to which her family first fled, Pakistan, educational deficiencies are noted by the author of the narrative – that Khatria only had access to interrupted schooling, so that the West is arranged in a hierarchical binary (Derrida cited in Youdell, 2005) with the 'Arab' world, which is deemed to be inferior in its treatment of women in comparison with the more progressive, wise and knowing West. This privileging educational discourse relies upon a citational chain that invokes images of an oppressive Islam in its treatment of women. Both Pakistan and the 'extremist' religious group, the Taliban, are invoked and tied up in this configuration, where 'Arab' society generally is represented in the citation as 'backward', 'strictly' religious, ignorant and 'evil'. As Butler (2004) suggests, in contemporary society, there is a tendency to situate 'Arab' persons as outside of what it means to be human, hence the suggestion in the narration that Khatria has enjoyed a lucky escape to the land of opportunity – Australia.

In this 'reading' of the data, I illustrate the subjectivities that are necessary for Khatria to take up in order to achieve recognition in her schooling milieu. In this sense, I illustrate the potential of ethnographic data to reveal the discourses that constrain student-subjects. However, I also acknowledge that my analysis is constrained by my own discursive choices and by the subjectivities that I, as a researcher, bring to the research and the ways I make these available to the reader. This understanding of methodology involves embracing what has elsewhere been described as 'the resistance to closure' which, in terms of a post-structural methodology, 'is both a choice and an inevitability: something to be both resigned and committed to' (Stronarch and MacLure, 1997: 5–6). Ultimately however,

I suggest that it is in 'unpacking' these discourses that a potential for educational change is realized, a point to which I return.

Bringing to light the workings of power, subjectivity and belonging

In the following section I continue to consider the power of post-structural ethnographic studies to trouble schooling exclusions. In a final analysis of ethnographic schooling data, I illustrate how schools are implicated in producing schooling exclusions, the power of post-structural ethnographies of schooling to bring these exclusionary practices to light and, in doing so, challenge their existence.

In the following vignette, I take up the story of Hanif who, like Khatria, is a student in Year 10 at Gundah High School. I explore the discourses within and against which a Muslim student in rural areas constructs his identity. Drawing on the work of Amanda Keddie (2007, 2011), particularly her arguments as they pertain to rurality and being Muslim, this vignette illustrates how rural schooling contexts are implicated in the making of 'hyper-normative' identities. By hyper-normative I mean the normative behaviours that are taken up to garner recognition, which, in this instance, are enhanced and amplified to increase the extent to which a student appears to be just like their schooling peers. I discuss how, in order to fit in, a Muslim student adopts the hetero-normative behaviours of his peer group at school (in direct contrast to his religious life at home), in order to be culturally recognizable. I also consider how this analysis might influence teaching practice in socially just ways.

The 'risky business' of belonging: In the playground, Gundah High School, Australia

The bell has rung, signalling an end to lunch and most of Year 10 are milling in the playground outside the school canteen waiting for their teachers to arrive at the hall for their Physical Education class. Students stand in small and larger groups talking. Hanif is in conversation with a blonde-haired girl, Rachel. They are talking about the upcoming Year 10 dance and who is likely to be voted 'Best [looking] Girl' and 'Best Arse'. Hanif tells Rachel that she will win Best Girl. She playfully shoves him away. A second girl, Annie, joins the conversation and Hanif tells Annie, while visibly turning to admire her bottom, that she too will win the 'Best Arse' category of the competition on the night.

When I later ask Hanif about this incident and, more particularly, about his relationship with Rachel, he tells me that he has no interest in

Post-structural ethnography

Rachel and that he was just playing around. He explains that his religion prevents him from having a girlfriend and that when the time is right, a marriage will be arranged for him by his parents. He also says that he will not be attending the school formal dance.

In this analysis I take up Butler's (1997) notion of 'recognition' to discuss the way students seek to be viable within normative frames of reference. In the playground scene outlined above, Hanif shows how the take up of hetero-normative behaviours can become a 'passport' to fitting in with his peers. To constitute himself as recognizable to his teenage friends, Hanif plays down his religious differences and takes up the secular and sexual discourses of his peers. In acts of flirting and coquetry with young (non-Muslim) girls that might be viewed as immodest in Islamic terms (contrary to *al-ihtisham*), (Mernissi, 1991 cited in Hamzeh and Oliver, 2010: 172), Hanif presents himself as just like the next guy at Gundah High School. Indeed, Hanif takes up discourses that associate 'successful masculinity' with 'laddish' accomplishment and gallantry (Keddie, 2007: 188). Noble suggests that exploring the spatial dimensions of how subjectivity is expressed in everyday, situated encounters means accounting for the way young Muslim men seek competence in relation to their place-based identities (2009). For Hanif, this seems to involve hyper-normative displays of masculinity that give him sub-cultural status (Youdell, 2003), but that sit in direct contrast to his religious beliefs about appropriate relations between the sexes. This 'dividing practice' (Foucault, 2002b), where Hanif is divided from those around him by his ethnicity and culture, subjugates the expression he is allowed to have of his ethnic and religious identity.

It could be argued that such behaviour is a direct consequence of gendered place relations. Hanif's take up of hyper-normative masculinity might be understood as a particularity of rural space, where gendered discourse has been argued to maintain established forms of traditional masculinity (Keddie, 2007). Bye suggests, for example, that in the rural, successful masculinity can depend on the performance of public displays of appropriate masculinities, such as the take up of 'intense masculine' displays (2009: 280). Wise (2010: 922) has also suggested that: 'embodiment of our social location manifests "in our actions, our modes of appearance and through a bodily *hexis* or bodily bearing – posture, manners, ways of speaking – for example" (Noble and Watkins, 2003: 522)'. For Hanif, doing gender appropriately in the rural appears to involve knowingly playing with discourses of courtship that he has no serious intention of taking up. Thus, in acts of limited agency, Hanif momentarily puts aside his religious beliefs and practices to attain peer recognition. To this end, while Hanif's values never appear to be seriously under threat, they are contested in socio-spatial terms. In the words of Bhatti, this is a 'risky business' (2006: 143), where belonging to a minority cultural group engenders behaviours that put at risk both one's values and one's take-up of a 'good' student identity.

Critical analysis of Hanif's behaviour reveals his sensitivity to the white cultural norms of his schooling environment against which he must pitch his identity. Drawing on these norms to constitute himself with power and agency, Hanif takes up a complex and contradictory position to acquire status and viability in his rural schooling milieu. These acts of positioning highlight the need for educators to be increasingly aware of the net of discourses that create and stifle identity possibilities for students. This involves educators being conscious both of their own discursive positioning, as well as of the discourses of gender, ethnicity, religion and space that weave together to construct and constrain the subjectivities of their students. This point highlights the need for teacher awareness of the subjectivities that constrain ethnic and cultural minority students. A pedagogy that privileges a false homogeneity needs to be replaced with a pedagogy responsive to heterogeneity in order to undo a schooling situation that privileges those students who come to school already equipped with identities that fit within existing normative discourses and practices of schooling. Critical recognition is needed of the unequal access children have to the dominant culture, and engagement is needed with pedagogies that question and challenge the very nature of this culture. Such a response is central to the goals of social justice in education.

Post-structural ethnography as a tool to unsettle schooling exclusions

What this chapter has shown to be absent in our schools is dialogue that deeply troubles and disrupts 'pedagogies of unbelonging' (Noble, 2005). Curricula and pedagogy that critically engage with prevailing discourses and subjugated knowledges has the potential to interrupt the hegemony and invisibility of these practices. Research methodologies that challenge and unsettle practices of subjectivation and the discourses that make these possible, of the sort I have demonstrated throughout this chapter, are part of a broader practice that can make explicit, as well as disrupt, schooling exclusions. Such an endeavour should consider the discursive repertoire in play in schooling spaces and its impact on schooling inclusions and exclusions. As Davies writes: 'poststructural theory enables a different sense of what is knowable, and of what can be done with that knowledge' (2004: 4). Post-structural ethnographies that construct counter-narratives of belonging might be taken up to encourage thinking around discourses of unbelonging and their points of resistance. Such work has the potential to transform education creatively in sustained and sustainable ways that reconfigure schooling environments in more socially just ways.

References

Bhatti, G. (2006) 'Ogbu and the debate on educational achievement: An exploration of the links between education, migration, identity and belonging'. *Intercultural Education*, 17 (2), 133–46.

Britzman, D.P. (1995) '"The question of belief": writing poststructural ethnography'. *Qualitative Studies in Education* 8 (3), 229–38.

Butler, J. (1997) *Excitable Speech: A politics of the performative*. New York: Routledge.

— (2004) *Precarious Life: The powers of mourning and violence*. London: Verso.

Bye, L.M. (2009) '"How to be a rural man": Young men's performances and negotiations of rural masculinities'. *Journal of Rural Studies*, 25, 278–88.

Choules, K. (2006) 'Globally privileged citizenship'. *Race Ethnicity and Education*, 9 (3), 275–93.

Davies, B. (2004) 'Introduction: Poststructural lines of flight in Australia'. *International Journal of Qualitative Studies in Education*, 17 (1), 1–9.

De Certeau, M. (1984) *The Practice of Everyday Life*. Berkeley: University of California Press.

Delamont, S. and Atkinson, P. (1995) *Fighting Familiarity: Essays on education and ethnography*. Cresskill, NJ: Hampton Press.

Denzin, N.K. and Lincoln, Y.S. (2000) 'Introduction: The discipline and practice of qualitative research'. In Denzin, N.K. and Lincoln, Y.S. (eds) *Handbook of Qualitative Research*. 2nd ed. Thousand Oaks, CA: Sage.

Foucault, M. (1998) *The Will to Knowledge*. London: Penguin. Vol. 1 of *The History of Sexuality*.

— (2000) 'Candidacy presentation, College de France, 1969'. In Rabinow, P. (ed.), *Ethics: Subjectivity and truth*. London: Penguin. Vol. 1 of *The Essential Works of Michel Foucault 1954–1984*.

— (2002a) 'Truth and juridical forms'. In Rabinow, P. (ed.), *Power*. London: Penguin. Vol. 3 of *The Essential Works Of Michel Foucault: 1954–1984*.

— (2002b) 'The subject and power'. In Rabinow, P. (ed.), *Power*. London: Penguin. Vol. 3 of *The Essential Works Of Michel Foucault: 1954–1984*.

Gilbert, R. and Gilbert, P. (1998) *Masculinity Goes to School*. Sydney: Allen and Unwin.

Gillborn, D. and Youdell, D. (2000) *Rationing Education: Policy, practice, reform and equity*. Buckingham: Open University Press.

— (2004) *Teacher, Tests and Triage: Standards, high-stakes testing and the rationing of education in the English classroom*. San Diego: American Educational Research Association.

Goldstein, T. (2008) 'Multiple commitments and ethical dilemmas in performed ethnography'. *Educational Insights*, 12 (2), 1–19.

Gordon, T., Holland, J. and Lahelma, E. (2001) 'Ethnographic research in educational settings'. In Atkinson, P., Coffey, A., Delamont, S., Lofland, J. and Lofland, L. (eds), *Handbook of Ethnography*. London: Sage.

Hamzeh, M.Z. and Oliver, K. (2010) 'Gaining research access into the lives of Muslim girls: Researchers negotiating *muslimness*, modesty, *inshallah*, and *haram*'. *International Journal of Qualitative Studies in Education*, 23 (2), 165–80.

Keddie, A. (2007) 'Games of subversion and sabotage: Issues of power, masculinity, class, rurality and schooling'. *British Journal of Sociology of Education*, 28 (2), 181–94.

— (2011) 'Supporting minority students through a reflexive approach to empowerment'. *British Journal of Sociology of Education*, 32 (2), 221–38.

Kenway, J., Kraack, A. and Hickey-Moody, A. (2006) *Masculinity beyond the Metropolis*. Basingstoke: Palgrave Macmillan.

Mac an Ghaill, M. (1988) *Young, Gifted and Black: Student–teacher relations in the schooling of black youth*. Milton Keynes: Open University Press.

Mernissi, F. (1991) *The Veil and the Male Elite: A feminist interpretation of women's rights in islam*. Trans. Lakeland, M.J. Cambridge, MA: Perseus Books.

Merriam, S.B., Johnson-Bailey, J., Lee, M., Kee, Y., Ntseane, G. and Muhamad, M. (2001) 'Power and positionality: Negotiating insider/outsider status within and across cultures'. *International Journal of Lifelong Education*, 20 (5), 405–16.

Noble, G. (2005) 'The discomfort of strangers: Racism, incivility and ontological security in a relaxed and comfortable nation'. *Journal of Intercultural Studies*, 26 (1), 107–20.

— (2009) '"Countless acts of recognition": Young men, ethnicity and the messiness of identities in everyday life'. *Social and Cultural Geography*, 10 (8), 875–91.

Noble, G. and Watkins, M. (2003) 'So, how did Bourdieu learn to play tennis? Habitus, consciousness and habituation'. *Cultural Studies*, 17 (3/4), 520–38.

Oikonomidoy, E. (2007) '"I see myself as a different person who [has] acquired a lot ...": Somali female students' journeys to belonging'. *Intercultural Education*, 18 (1), 15–27.

Popoviciu, L., Haywood, C. and Mac an Ghaill, M. (2006) 'The promise of post-structuralist methodology: ethnographic representation of education and masculinity'. *Ethnography and Education*, 1 (3), 393–412.

Rasmussen, M.L. and Harwood, V. (2003) 'Performativity, youth and injurious speech'. *Teaching Education*, 14 (1), 25–36.

Rhedding-Jones, J. (1996) 'Researching early schooling: Poststructural practices and academic writing in an ethnography'. *British Journal of Sociology of Education*, 17 (1), 21–37.

Scott, D. and Usher, R. (1999) *Researching Education: Data, methods and theory in educational enquiry*. London: Cassell.

Spindler, G. (ed.) (1982) *Doing the Ethnography of Schooling: Educational anthropology in action*. New York: Holt, Rinehart and Winston.

St Pierre, E.A. and Pillow, W.S. (2000) *Working the Ruins: Feminist poststructural theory and methods in education*. New York: Routledge.

Stronach, I. and MacLure, M. (1997) *Educational Research Undone: The postmodern embrace*. Buckingham: Open University Press.

Subreenduth, S. and Rhee, J. (2010) 'A porous, morphing, and circulatory mode of self–other: Decolonizing identity politics by engaging transnational reflexivity'. *International Journal of Qualitative Studies in Education*, 23 (3), 331–46.

Thomson, P. (2002) *Schooling the Rustbelt Kids: Making the difference in changing times*. Sydney: Allen and Unwin.

Willis, P.E. (1977) *Learning to Labour: How working class kids get working class jobs*. New York: Colombia University Press.

Wise, A. (2010) 'Sensuous multiculturalism: Emotional landscapes of inter-ethnic living in Australian suburbia'. *Journal of Ethnic and Migration Studies*, 36 (6), 917–37.

Youdell, D. (2003) 'Identity traps or how black students fail: The interactions between biographical, sub-cultural, and learner identities'. *British Journal of Sociology of Education*, 24 (1), 3–20.

— (2005) 'Sex–gender–sexuality: How sex, gender and sexuality constellations are constituted in secondary schools'. *Gender and Education*, 17 (3), 249–70.

— (2006a) *Impossible Bodies, Impossible Selves: Exclusions and student subjectivities*. Dordrecht: Springer.

— (2006b) 'Subjectivation and performative politics – Butler thinking Althusser and Foucault: Intelligibility, agency and the raced-nationed-religioned subjects of education'. *British Journal of Sociology of Education*, 27 (4), 511–28.

— (2011) *School Trouble: Identity, power and politics in education*. London: Routledge.

Chapter 4

Being a socio-professional insider-researcher in Pakistan: Possibilities and challenges for educational research

Saeeda Shah

Introduction

Globalization, the communications explosion, economic universalism and international mobility have caused demographic changes worldwide. Communities are becoming increasingly complex and diverse and this brings new challenges for qualitative researchers. For insider-researchers, the interplay between contextual dynamics and the researcher's identity adds a further dimension to the research process. The literature on research methodology demands a shift from 'researching upon' to 'researching with', and the reconsideration of the subjectivities and power relations between researcher and researched. The ongoing debates about the positive and negative influence of researchers in qualitative research draw attention to the complexities of the role of the 'insider-researcher'.

This chapter contributes to the existing body of literature by drawing upon my personal experiences of doing research in Pakistan as an insider-researcher. As a Muslim female academic of Pakistani origin who worked in higher education in Pakistan for about two decades, I could be broadly positioned as an insider, both socially and professionally. However, a number of factors including my socio-economic class, my family background (which is of significance in Pakistani society), an education obtained abroad, and a role as an academic in a UK university, intersect with my positioning as an insider. Thus, there are significant potential implications for me as researcher.

In this chapter I discuss the concept of insider-researcher and its situated constructions and interpretations. This is followed by a discussion of the advantages and disadvantages of being an insider-researcher and the implications for the generation and analysis of data. I argue that no one is an absolute insider-researcher or outsider-researcher and that a researcher's positioning and identity is constructed at the intersections of multiple dynamics. However, while having particular insider characteristics in particular research situations can facilitate research, it is important to recognize and acknowledge the inherent complexities and challenges.

Who is an insider?

The insider–outsider debate has been the focus of much scholarly work. Early anthropologists researching 'other' locations and cultures constructed insider–outsider as a dichotomy, with the defining parameters being 'local' and 'stranger'. Insiderness in such cases has been defined by membership of a particular community or group. However, there is a growing realization that the distinction between the outsider and the insider is ambiguous and arbitrary, and therefore, explaining it as a simple dichotomy is problematic. Even within close-knit communities and tribes, individuals can be outsiders or insiders with respect to age, gender, education, profession, economic status, power and many other factors. Therefore, each case needs to be critiqued and explained in its uniqueness.

Ethnographers or anthropologists who spend time among the communities that they research can develop deep and detailed knowledge of these social contexts. However, their position is different from that of an insider-researcher who is 'someone whose biography (gender, race, class, sexual orientation and so on) gives her [sic] a lived familiarity with the group being researched' (Griffith, 1998: 361). In contrast, an outsider-researcher is 'a researcher who does not have any intimate knowledge of the group being researched, prior to entry into the group' (Griffith, 1998: 361). This distinction is based upon an assumption of a broadly homogeneous group bestowed with a more or less fixed identity. However, the factors that define a group and its membership can be relative, fluid, multiple, situational and contingent. Often we are all insiders and outsiders moving 'back and forth across different boundaries' (Griffith, 1998: 368). Therefore, people can be both insiders and outsiders at the same time and in the same context. DeVault argues that identities are 'always relative, cross cut by other differences and often situational and contingent' (1996: 35). Some features of the researcher's identity, such as sex, ethnicity, race and colour are innate and unchanging, while there are multiple other features that are extrinsic, acquired, learned or evolving. They shape and shift the positionalities of researchers and researched on an insider–outsider continuum. A researcher is constructed as an insider or outsider not only by self-definition, but also by the research participants themselves.

Researcher identities in qualitative research shape an investigation and its findings because, due to the very nature of this type of inquiry, data are explained and interpreted, and knowledge is constructed through interaction and interpretation. The insider-researcher may have the advantage of a deeper understanding of the research context and is therefore in a position to present an informed picture of the issues under investigation. The outsider-researcher, on the one hand, may face difficulties in gaining consent from participants or access to data sources. While limited knowledge of the context may hinder the creation of a robust account of the phenomenon being researched, it may offer a more impartial interpretation based directly on the data provided by the interviewees. It is simplistic to label one type of research better than the other. Within their own specific limitations, both insider and outsider-researchers have possibilities and problems that contribute to the body of knowledge about research.

The nature of the relationships between the researcher and the research participants has implications for the meaningfulness, credibility and robustness of the data in qualitative research. An interview is a 'social event' (Hammersley and Atkinson, 1983: 126), and is determined by discursive relations and situatedness. *Who* does the research has effects on data collection and analysis. The researcher and the participants jointly contribute to this knowledge-building activity, drawing on their respective understandings of social systems and awareness of each other's subjectivities as mutually constructed. Therefore, a good rapport between interviewees and interviewer is vital for qualitative research (Creswell, 2003; Denscombe, 2007) because it may lead to the generation of trustworthy and in-depth data. The insider-researcher, being a part of the context, may have the participants' trust and confidence. Taylor defines insiderness as 'a contemporary cultural space with which the researcher has regular and ongoing contact; where the researcher's personal relationships are deeply embedded in the field ... and where the researcher is privy to undocumented historical knowledge of the people and cultural phenomenon being studied' (2011: 9). Roulston points out that 'interactional problems are sometimes ascribed to the interviewer's inability to understand and orient to participants in ways that facilitate mutual understanding' (2013: 2). Not being a member of the social or language group can contribute to a lack of understanding about the sensitivity of topics and how these should be approached.

The insider-researcher in the field

The researcher, being a social researcher, cannot be separated from the social enquiry (Hammersley and Atkinson, 1995). Hammersley and Atkinson argue that one should 'abandon the idea that the social character of research can be "standardized out" or avoided by becoming a "fly on the wall" or "full participant"'(1995: 19). This argument constructs the role of the qualitative investigator as a participant in the research process. If qualitative researchers recognize their role as social investigators, this self-awareness has the potential to produce insightful, critical, systematic and skilful accounts (Morrison, 2007).

Admittedly, insider-researchers have certain advantages as well as disadvantages in conducting research (Edwards, 2002). Because of the specific nature of qualitative research, the insider-researcher may benefit from previously established friendships and relationships in gaining access to the field as well as gaining the confidence and trust of the participants. Foster, interviewing black women, emphasizes the 'positive effect that a shared identity can have on establishing rapport and gaining authentic accounts' (1994: 136). Mirza (1995) highlights the importance of drawing on the normal ground rules of reciprocity and trust that pertain to social interaction in the community. Finch (1984) illustrates how a researcher can draw on personal knowledge of a situation, as she did in her interviews with the wives of clergymen. These interviews were informed by her own experience of being married to a clergyman at that time.

While contact with the research context and knowledge of the local social systems and norms are helpful in arranging and conducting field work, researchers also argue that 'Familiarity with the setting or previous acquaintance with the participants dulls the researcher's ability to view the setting with the sensitivity one would have when seeing it for the first time' (Morse, 1994: 27). Haw, writing about her research in a state school, admits that 'my criticality was blunted by my familiarity and consequent assumptions' (1996: 323). Hitchcock and Hughes advise the researcher to be careful not to become 'so involved that she ceases to be an observer and remains only a participant' (1991, 37). Describing his own experience of researching shared governance at the university where he worked, Labaree underlined the need to navigate the 'hidden ethical and methodological dilemmas of insiderness' (2002: 109). Malone argues that 'the most dangerous and difficult place to attempt qualitative research is in a familiar institutional setting' (2003: 812).

Qualitative researchers understand the importance of building trust with interviewees (Creswell, 2003; Denscombe, 2007; Johnson, 2001), emphasizing that 'the quality of responses [could] considerably depend' not only upon 'getting in' or 'gaining access' but also upon 'getting on' with the respondents or 'achieving social access' (Shah, 2004: 559). In reflecting on the experience of interviewing college heads in Pakistan, I acknowledge that:

> How they [the interviewees] might have constructed me as a researcher in view of their knowledge of me, cannot be denied to have affected their responses. Also, my understanding and interpretation of their responses cannot be viewed as dis-embedded from my prior knowledge and experience.
>
> (Shah, 1998: 158)

Understanding and interpreting information through the lens of the socio-professional insider is inescapable for the insider-researcher. When a colleague mentioned she had refused an offer of a principalship away from her hometown, I could understand the cultural pressures and extended family responsibilities that underpinned her decision. Similarly, when another colleague mentioned having to depend on male clerks in banks and male-dominated central accounts offices, and having to tolerate the malpractices of these male clerks, I could identify the cultural norms in that segregated Muslim society that constrained these professional women. While on the positive side, this knowledge and understanding might facilitate meaning-making and insight, it can be also argued that this closeness might hinder criticality when researching 'familiar and taken for granted phenomena' (Shah, 2004: 556). In this respect, being reflective, transparent (Rubin and Rubin, 2005) explicit, honest, and accountable (Oancea and Furlong, 2007) are some essential measures for research validity and trustworthiness. The insider-researcher also has an ethical and social responsibility. Some scholars emphasize the importance of not betraying the participants' trust in any way (Busher and James, 2007; van Deventer, 2009) as it may cause difficulties for subsequent researchers. Furthermore, the data collected by a trusted insider may lead to tensions between responsibility to the research and responsibility to the participants. Glesne draws attention to this challenge, commenting that 'when others trust you, you invariably receive the privilege and burden of learning things that are problematic at best and dangerous at worst' (1999: 119).

Another aspect to be acknowledged is the impact of the insider-researcher on the data generated. It is simplistic to assume that an insider has the perfect perspective on the respective context. Even the data generated by two similarly positioned insider-researchers may lead to findings that are completely different. Wolcott emphasizes this point, arguing that 'There is no monolithic insider view', maintaining that 'every view *is a* way of seeing, not *the* way of seeing' (1999: 137). How a qualitative researcher relates to the world under investigation and what he or she comes to know cannot be disconnected from the researcher and the contextual dynamics. Elsewhere I have argued that:

> What the interviewee wishes to convey, what the interviewer learns, and how it is interpreted are influenced by the respective subjectivities of the participants and the complex forces present within that context. Face-to-face responses are not simply given to the questions, but to the researcher who poses those questions, in interplay with how the participants perceive the researcher and themselves in that social context.
>
> (Shah 2004: 552)

It is important that an insider-researcher considers all these aspects carefully and engages in critical reflection and reflexivity. Morrison explains the notion of 'reflexivity' as 'the process by which researchers come to understand how they are positioned in relation to the knowledge they are producing' (2007: 32). Reflexivity rejects the likelihood of investigators constantly attaining a completely objective perspective with reference to research because the researchers are part of the social, political and educational worlds that they are investigating. Therefore, with reference to reflexivity, investigators need to take into account 'that "the sense" they make of the world is reflected in, and affected by, the norms and values that have been absorbed as part of life experience' (Morrison, 2007: 32). The need for reflexivity and a 'critical eye' increases for an insider-researcher because of his/her familiarity and closeness to the context. An important source for developing criticality and reflexivity in my case has been critical debates with researchers from different socio-cultural backgrounds. For example, during my first round of interviewing in Pakistan, I was accompanied by a colleague from the UK (a white woman academic) who wished to do some data collection in Pakistan for her own research. This was her first visit to Pakistan, which she described as completely different from her previous social repertoire. Our informal discussions and conversations as two researchers with diverse socio-cultural orientations and different experiences facilitated our critical reflections on the research process. Engaging with research in different countries also enhances criticality and reflexivity. In my case, besides doing research in Pakistan, I have conducted research in the UK as well as in

Russia. My experience is that conducting research in different countries, societies and cultures helps develop a critical eye and encourages reflexivity.

Being an insider-researcher

In this section I discuss my experience of doing research in Pakistan with reference to two studies that have a specific focus on face-to-face interviewing and the effects of being a social and professional insider. Besides being a Muslim academic woman of Pakistani origin with extensive experience of working in higher education in Pakistan, I also have extended family networks and active professional links in Pakistan, and visit the country regularly. All this makes me a social and professional insider in many ways. The interview data for the two above-mentioned studies were collected from senior educational leaders in Pakistan. The participants in the first study were 31 women and men college-heads from one specific region in Pakistan: 11 interviewees were women and 20 were men (this is discussed further later in this section). The second study involved interviews with five female vice chancellors in Pakistan. These interviews explored the views and experiences of these senior leaders in depth and elicited detailed narrations of their personal experiences as women vice chancellors in a predominantly segregated traditional Muslim society. The research focus was on career trajectories of women vice chancellors in Pakistan, the challenges in accessing and maintaining top leadership positions, and the barriers and enablers from the professional, structural, social and religious domains.

My being a socio-professional insider facilitated access to the field. The first woman vice chancellor whom I interviewed was a colleague and also a good friend. When I explained my research to her, she facilitated the organization of interviews with other women vice chancellors and provided their contact details and private phone numbers. I used her office to contact these women and make interview arrangements. The fact that I was an academic colleague of Pakistani origin with experience of working in universities in Pakistan as well as a friend of their colleague, facilitated access to the field.

The data collected from these women vice chancellors were rich and detailed. They shared their life histories and personal facts that had influenced their career trajectories and decisions. They would often refer to their experiences as women academics, knowing that I had also worked in a senior position in Pakistan before leaving for the UK. I was an insider who understood the professional and the cultural systems. However, at the same time I was an outsider who had come from the UK to conduct the research and I would be returning – I was no longer a permanent presence in the local professional space. They might not have provided some of these details if I were a colleague sharing the professional space with them.

Qualitative research data do not exist independently of the researcher; it is the result of the interaction between the researcher and the participants (Gummesson, 2003). Interviewing is much more than 'a conversation with a purpose' (Mason, 2002; Ribbins, 2007). Every interview is unique, and the researcher must be prepared to adapt to its uniqueness (Rubin and Rubin, 2005). According to Chase (2005: 657), 'a narrative is a joint production of narrator and listener' and narratives are generated and constructed on the spot, during the interview, instead of being collected as pre-existing facts (Elliot, 2005). This construction of knowledge during the interaction is influenced by the researcher's role and position as well as the interactional dynamics. Being a social insider offers access to relevant social cues and interactional devices that assist in the management of 'the complex nature of interaction' (Denscombe, 2007: 174). However, identity constructions in the interview situation and interactional dynamics also play an equally significant role.

In my research in a complex socio-cultural setting, being a socio-professional insider proved useful, not only for designing the research, attaining access, and planning field work, but also for the interactional dynamics that later informed the analysis. My knowledge of the social and professional contexts and of the patterns of experience therein, as well as my membership of the same speech community, not only facilitated the conduct and logistics of data collection but also enriched conversations, adding to the quality of the data collected. Merton and Kendall claim that a researcher, through 'familiarity with the situation is able to recognize symbolic or functional silences, distortions, avoidance or blocking, [and] he/she is the more prepared to explore implications' (in Cohen and Manion, 1994: 290). Jorgensen emphasizes familiarity with the research context and considers it 'impossible to acquire more than a very crude notion of the insider's world, for instance, until you comprehend the language and culture that is used to communicate its meaning' (1989: 14). This is particularly relevant with regard to undocumented knowledge, 'social cues' and 'interactional devices' such as social norms for any interactional context including choice of words, voice, intonation and body language which, when used appropriately, can facilitate interaction and research. Irvine *et al.* emphasize that 'insider researchers have a repertoire of "social cues" at their disposal which they can use to facilitate research' (2013: 87).

My lived experience of the research context, belonging to the same speech community, and sharing the same broader culture and religion enabled me to understand and interpret the responses. Foster's argument for enhanced understanding of the problems and possibilities 'when researcher and researched are members of the same cultural and speech community' (1994: 131) is relevant. Being a Pakistani academic, I was a social and professional insider, even though I admit that in each interview situation, I might have been an outsider in different ways as well. This affirms the earlier argument that we are all insiders and outsiders in different ways. Furthermore, there is no denying the issues that concern a colleague-turned-researcher, the political and social problems linked with familiarity and role change, and their effects on research. The fact that I was an insider, researching colleagues' experiences, made me doubly anxious and responsible for preserving their anonymity and confidentiality so as not to cause them any harm or even embarrassment even when my participants did not express any concerns about it: 'I certainly did not look forward to hearing complaints from my colleagues on breach of trust, on my return to work' (Shah, 1998: 166).

In the reporting of insider-research, it is vital that the interview situation is made explicit because the context 'is intrinsic to understanding any data that are obtained' (Silverman, 1985: 162). Data collection for my first study coincided with a five-week visit to Pakistan, which also entailed many personal and family commitments. The geographical region of focus for that research consisted of four districts in a mountain region with poor quality roads. My being an insider both professionally and socially had its advantages because I was able to organize data collection through professional contacts and colleagues. The amazing speed at which the interview times were agreed upon with busy college heads, and the manner in which the 31 interviews were arranged and conducted within a period of fewer than 30 working days in four different districts scattered over a hilly area of 11,000 square miles, would not have been manageable for a social or professional outsider. My insider's knowledge, particularly when supported by positional power and social contacts, facilitated my fieldwork by mitigating the issues of access through an informed manipulation of resources. However, this also raises issues concerning the validity of the data collected by an insider-researcher:

- how much the respondents may not tell because he or she makes assumptions about the researcher's knowledge as an insider
- how much the researcher may fail to ask, believing it to be too obvious or too insignificant: nearness blunting the criticality.

Insider-researcher

My socio-professional positioning and the power–knowledge distribution as perceived by the participants provided further challenges. For a trustworthy and participative research context, it is important that the participants feel valued and empowered. This requires the interaction between participants and researcher to be 'free from all constraints of domination, whether their source be conscious strategic behaviour or communication barriers secured in ideology and neurosis' (Habermas, 1976: xvii). This means a constant manoeuvring of positions in order to satisfy the methodological needs of the research. Being an insider offered me opportunities to use my social knowledge in a number of ways. For example, I had arranged an interview with a local female college head. However, the evening before, the opportunity arose to travel to nearby district headquarters where it would be possible to interview three or four principals. I decided to avail myself of that opportunity and I cancelled the planned interview, leaving my colleague a message of explanation. How far it is appropriate to cancel a pre-arranged interview by leaving a message, and how it might affect a researcher's relationship with his/her informants is not clear. However, I acted in the confidence that my colleague, on the basis of our social and professional relationship, would be sympathetic to this change of schedule.

However, being an insider can also lead to the imposition of restrictions and controls. For example, for my travels to be socially and culturally acceptable in a region where I was known to most professionals, I needed to make appropriate travel arrangements because it is not deemed culturally appropriate for a woman of my background to be alone with a male for the length of time required for a qualitative interview. Ganesh mentions the issue of 'avoiding interviewing men alone' (1993: 133) during her research in India and refers to the 'problem of suitable space for interviewing men' (1993: 135). This points to wider regional cultural norms with regard to gender. However, conducting the interview in an open place, with the possibility of interruptions did not suit the recording requirements. I needed to manage this complication within the social, as well as the methodological frameworks. The female colleague from the UK who had accompanied me to Pakistan for the purposes of her own research was staying with me. I decided to ask her to chaperone my interviews with the male participants. Her presence during the one-to-one interviews with them would satisfy the local cultural norms. Additionally, because she did not understand Urdu – the language in which the interviews were conducted – confidentiality would not be compromised. This proved a useful arrangement because it complied with social norms and maintained methodological rigour. The respondents were visibly relaxed when assured

51

that my colleague did not know Urdu. While the interviewees switched to English occasionally to involve her socially, they readily reverted to Urdu when the participants did not wish her to follow the conversation. Another aspect of this arrangement that I had not anticipated was that my white colleague, being a researcher herself, was *observing* the interaction even if not following the conversation. I realized this when, after the first such interview, she started asking me questions about the seating arrangement, paralinguistic cues and social elements (tea and snacks being served before the interviews, etc.). This led to interesting discussions between the two of us as she said that she had learned a lot about the cultural aspects of researching in Pakistan. Her questions and comments made me reflect on these elements, providing yet another lens through which to engage with the process.

Contextual forces and cultural systems in certain situations can be strong determining factors in fieldwork. However, an insider can also manipulate these systems, as occasionally happened during my data collection. For example, I went to interview a female college head in a different district and was accompanied by a local female colleague. An opportunity arose to interview a local male college head. He came to the female principal's office that had been made available for the interview. During the interview, my host female colleague casually walked in twice to indicate that I was appropriately accompanied. The second situation was when a male college head came to be interviewed at my female cousin's house where I was staying. He brought along a male colleague, which is an appropriate practice when visiting a woman's house. The compulsion to observe cultural norms determined not just the female insider-researcher's conduct but also the male participant's social behaviour.

Being a Pakistani, Muslim, academic, I shared these broad categories with all my participants. However, in the case of male participants, sex became a category of difference. The need to maintain appropriate gender relations added a significant dimension to methodological considerations. The twenty male participants I interviewed all offered to come to my office or my home. They spared their time, paid their own travel expenses (refusing to accept reimbursement), and in some cases, travelled long distances by public or private transport to come to meet me. Why these busy principals chose to come to be interviewed at the requested place and time needs to be understood in the socio-political context, taking into account the researcher's position within that context, the associated gender discourses and culturally-appropriate patterns of behaviour. With my knowledge of the local cultural norms, I was able to move flexibly between discourses of gender, professional positioning, and family background, depending on what suited the pragmatics and constraints. I cordially accepted the male participants' offers to come for interviews, except in the case of two who worked in colleges in remote hilly areas, when in view of the travelling facilities at my disposal, it saved time to go there myself. However, I had to make culturally appropriate travel arrangements so as not to offend them. As almost all the research participants knew me and my family, I had to be very careful to conduct myself appropriately. That meant being accompanied, keeping my head covered when among men, keeping an appropriate distance from male colleagues when meeting them, using appropriate linguistic and paralinguistic signals, and observing appropriate cultural patterns of behaviour.

When interviewing women college heads, I opted to visit their offices or homes despite their offers to come to me. My going to them was, in that socio-cultural context, an acknowledgement of their value as research participants, and this contributed to their confidence and sense of empowerment. Second, being an insider, I knew that in spite of being senior leaders, these college heads would face difficulties in making culturally appropriate travel arrangements. Travelling for women is subject to local cultural constraints, although there are variations across classes, areas, families, and sub-groups. This is in keeping with the preferred practice in Muslim societies that, while travelling, women should be accompanied by an appropriate female or a male *mehram*, a common practice among middle-class families in the region. Besides a husband in the case of a married woman, other *mehrams* include all those males with whom marriage cannot take place according to the Islamic sharia, such as father, brother, son or grandfather. Informed by insider knowledge of complex social sub-systems operating in the local culture, I carefully avoided exposing the women principals to the inconvenience and constraints of travelling, and chose mutually convenient places to meet them for interviews.

I was able to draw on my insider's repertoire of social skills during the interviews. For example, when I visited a female principal in her office, colleagues would gather, sometimes in large groups, to pay courtesy calls. It would have been culturally inappropriate for the host principal in that context to ask them to leave us alone for the purpose of interviewing. However, as a guest, I would use these situations to my advantage but without offending my hosts' cultural sensibilities. A guest can be excused at times for infringing behavioural norms. For example, I interviewed one principal in her office after having explained to the group of gathered colleagues the need for privacy. They left politely. However, a few minutes later, one of them re-entered the office, interrupting the interview and attempting to answer on behalf of the principal.[1] To give her a reason to leave the room, I requested her to show my accompanying colleague around the college. However, she soon returned, having handed the responsibility over to another colleague. Soon the principal began passing the questions over to her to answer, choosing to remain silent. It was an awkward situation and contrary to my intentions. Finally, I had to tell the intruder in clear but pleasant tones that her presence was in violation of my research procedures. Such a request by the host principal would have been considered impolite and would have led to staff–management problems later. I, however, was positioned differently within this relationship. Although I had a guest's obligation, which certainly did not allow me to be rude to the host staff, I also had a guest's prerogative. I was able to draw on my knowledge of the socio-cultural norms in Pakistan without offending them.

Conclusion

Conducting qualitative interviews is complex and challenging in every context. A great many factors affect interaction between the interviewer and interviewee with the insider–outsider status of the researcher being one such factor. Interviewing in culturally diverse contexts, however, presents even more complex challenges because in the majority of cases, researchers are likely to be cultural outsiders who do not share the cultural knowledge or cultural practices of their participants. They may well struggle to gain access to the field or to engage in interactions that elicit meaningful, detailed and rich data. However, it is simplistic to assume that being a social insider ensures cultural knowledge and sensitivity in all research contexts. Individuals from similar cultural backgrounds vary in myriad ways. For example being a member of the same ethnic group may not necessarily facilitate access or the building of trust, because there may be other issues such as gender or social class that override the advantages of a researcher coming from the same ethnic group as their participants. On the other hand, in some South Asian societies there is a strong tradition of hospitality that accommodates the requests of a guest, even if the guest happens to be a stranger. In my case, even though I was a social and professional insider in Pakistan, each interview situation had its own dynamics and demanded a flexible approach. Generalizations regarding the advantages or disadvantages of being an insider or outsider-researcher are problematic, and at times, misleading.

It is important that all researchers who interview in culturally diverse contexts demonstrate cultural sensitivity and are prepared to become learners by familiarizing themselves with the cultural context before they approach potential participants and before they conduct interviews. An ignorance of the broader social context where research is to be carried out can be a barrier to generating valid data. Secondly, in the absence of any understanding of cultural context and social phenomenon, a researcher may make assumptions that are invalid. What is important for all researchers, insiders and outsiders – and we are all insiders and outsiders at the same time and in different ways – is to understand the context of an interview and its patterns of interaction, and to recognize how power potentially shapes both the interview process and the resulting data. A good researcher, be they insider or outsider, will constantly reflect upon and adjust how he or she approaches research practice.

References

Bhatti, G. (1995) 'A journey into the unknown: Ethnographic study of Asian children'. In Griffiths, M. and Troyna, B. (eds) *Antiracism, Culture and Social Justice in Education*. Stoke-on-Trent: Trentham Books, 20–32.

Busher, H. and James, N. (2007) 'Ethics of research in education'. In Briggs, A. and Coleman, M. (eds) *Research Methods in Educational Leadership and Management*. 2nd ed. London: Paul Chapman, 106–22.

Chase, S. (2005) 'Narrative Inquiry: Multiple lenses, approaches, voices'. In Denzin, N. and Lincoln, Y. (eds) *The Sage Handbook of Qualitative Research*. 3rd ed. Thousand Oaks, CA: Sage Publications, 651–79.

Cohen, L. and Manion, L. (1994) *Research Methods in Education*. London: Routledge.

Creswell, J. (2003) *Research Design: Qualitative, quantitative, and mixed methods approaches*. London: Sage Publications.

Denscombe, M. (2007) *The Good Research Guide: For small-scale social research projects*. Open University Press.

DeVault, M.L. (1996) 'Talking back to sociology: Distinctive contributions of feminist methodology'. *Annual Review of Sociology*, 22, 29–50.

Edwards, B. (2002) 'Deep insider research'. *Qualitative Research Journal*, 2 (1), 71–84.

Elliot, J. (2005) *Using Narrative in Social Research: Qualitative and quantitative approaches*, London and Thousand Oaks, CA: Sage Publications.

Finch, J. (1984) '"It's great to have someone to talk to": The ethics and politics of interviewing women'. In Bell, C. and Roberts, H. (eds) *Social Researching: Politics, problems, practice*. London: Routledge and Kegan Paul, 70–86.

Foster, M. (1994) 'The power to know one thing is never the power to know all things'. In Giltin, A. (ed.) *Power and Method: Political activism and educational research*. New York and London: Routledge, 129–46.

Ganesh, K. (1993) 'Breaching the Wall of Difference'. In Bell, D., Caplan, P. and Karim, W.J. (eds) *Gendered Fields: Women, men and ethnography*. London: Routledge, 128–42.

Glesne, C. (1999) *Becoming Qualitative Researchers: An introduction*. 2nd ed. New York: Longman.

Griffith, A.I. (1998) 'Insider/outsider: Epistemological privilege and mothering work'. *Human Studies*, 21, 361–76.

Gummesson, E. (2003) 'All research is interpretive!'. *Journal of Business & Industrial Marketing*, 18 (6/7), 482–92.

Habermas J. (1976) *Legitimation Crisis*. Boston: Beacon Press.

Hammersley, M. and Atkinson, P. (1983) *Ethnography: Principles in practice*. London: Tavistock.

— (1995) *Ethnography: Principles in practice*. 2nd ed. London: Routledge.

Haw, K. (1996) 'Exploring the educational experiences of Muslim girls: Tales told to tourists – should the white researcher stay at home?'. *British Educational Research Journal*, 22 (3), 319–30.

Hitchcock, G. and Hughes, D. (1991) *Research and the Teacher: A qualitative introduction to school-based research*. London: Routledge.

Irvine, A., Drew, P. and Sainsbury, R. (2013) '"Am I not answering your questions properly?" Clarification, adequacy and responsiveness in semi-structured telephone and face-to-face interviews'. *Qualitative Research*, 13 (1), 87–106.

Johnson, J. (2001) 'In-depth interviewing'. In Gubrium, J.F. and Holstein, J.A. (eds) *Handbook of Interview Research: Context and method*, Thousand Oaks, CA: Sage Publications, 103–20.

Jorgensen, D.L. (1989) *Participant Observation: A methodology for human studies*. Newbury Park, CA: Sage.

Labaree, R.V. (2002) 'The risk of "going observationalist": Negotiating the hidden dilemmas of being an insider participant observer'. *Qualitative Research*, 2 (1), 97–122.

Malone, S. (2003) 'Ethics at home: Informed consent in your own backyard'. *International Journal of Qualitative Studies in Education*, 16 (6), 797–815.

Mason, J. (2002) *Qualitative Researching*. London: Sage.

Merton R.K. and Kendall P.L. (1946) 'The focused interview'. *American Journal of Sociology*. 51: 541–57.

Mirza, M. (1995) 'Some ethical dilemmas in field work: Feminist and antiracist methodologies'. In Griffiths, M. and Troyna, B. (eds) *Antiracism, Culture and Social Justice in Education*. Stoke-on-Trent: Trentham Books, 163–81.

Morrison, M. (2007) 'What do we mean by educational research?'. In Briggs, A. and Coleman, M. (eds) *Research Methods in Educational Leadership and Management*. Los Angeles and London: Sage, 13–36.

Morse, J.M. (1994) 'Emerging from the data'. In Morse, J.M. (ed.) *Critical Issues in Qualitative Research Methods*. Thousand Oaks, CA: Sage Publications, 23–43.

Oancea, A. and Furlong, J. (2007) 'Expressions of excellence and the assessment of applied and practice-based research'. *Research Papers in Education*, 22 (2), 119–37.

Ribbins, P. (2007) 'Interviews in educational research: Conversations with a purpose'. In Briggs, A. and Coleman, M. (eds) *Research Methods in Educational Leadership and Management*. Los Angeles and London: Sage, 207–23.

Roulston, K. (2013) 'Interactional problems in research interviews'. *Qualitative Research*, 8 February 2013, 1–17. Online. http://qrj.sagepub.com/content/early/2013/01/28/1468794112473497.full.pdf (requires subscription).

Rubin, H.J. and Rubin, I.S. (2005) *Qualitative Interviewing: The art of hearing data*. London and Thousand Oaks, CA: Sage.

Shah, S. (1998) 'Educational management: Practices of college heads in Pakistan', Unpublished PhD thesis, University of Nottingham.

— (2004) 'Researcher in cross-cultural context: A social intruder'. *British Educational Research Journal*, 30 (4), 549–75.

Silverman, D. (1985) *Qualitative Methodology and Sociology*. Aldershot: Gower.

Taylor, J. (2011) 'The intimate insider: Negotiating the ethics of friendship when doing insider research'. *Qualitative Research*, 11 (3), 3–22.

Van Deventer, J.P. (2009) 'Ethical considerations during human-centred overt and covert research'. *Quality and Quantity*, 43, 45–57.

Wolcott, H. (1999) 'Ethnography: A way of seeing'. Walnut Creek, CA: Altamira Press.

Endnotes

[1] Some interesting interview situations, when researching with British Asian communities, are mentioned by Bhatti (1995) and Mirza (1995).

Chapter 5
Overcoming barriers in researching diversity
Geri Smyth

Introduction
This chapter draws from three research projects conducted by the author to discuss approaches to educational research with diverse populations. It highlights some of the barriers that may be encountered when the researchers are from a linguistic and cultural majority and in a position of relative power to the researched. It also discusses the potential effects of power when the research is with children from minority populations and when the topic being researched is attitudes to diversity. The chapter is specifically concerned with designing research that will empower linguistic and cultural minority participants, and stresses the importance of relationships of trust between researcher and researched.

The first project used 'open space technology' with young people to discuss their understandings of diversity (Allan *et al.*, 2009). The second used digital photography to access the perspectives towards education of young people whose first language differed from the language of education (Smyth, 2006) and the third project investigated, through participatory research, the experiences of refugee adults trying to negotiate access to their profession in a new country and language (Kum *et al.*, 2008).

In all three projects the researchers were aware of the differences in power, language and ethnicity and sought methods that would give voice to the researched while also offering strategies to develop their skills or social networks. The chapter outlines the approaches taken in each project and presents samples of the data collected to support the subsequent discussion around empowerment and cultural relevance. The benefits and barriers of each approach are considered, along with whether the methods are appropriate and applicable across age, gender and socioeconomic status.

Educational research with minority populations
Most of the educational research conducted with linguistic and cultural minority populations is concerned with equity and social justice in schooling outcomes. This research has been conducted mainly by linguistic

majority academics in positions of relative power vis-à-vis the groups being researched. There is a danger that this situation can lead to key issues being missed, invalid research instruments and erroneous analysis of the data. Disciplines other than education, such as community work, nursing, medicine, psychology and social work have also explored issues around majority research with minority populations and we can draw from these other disciplines in developing approaches in educational research.

The values, initial approaches and methodologies in research design need to be examined. Meleis (1996) has proposed eight criteria for culturally competent research from a nursing science perspective. These provide useful discussion points for educational research as they underpin the values of a socially just education, and are summarized below:

- *Contextuality*: an understanding of the sociocultural, political and historical context of where the study participants live
- *Relevance*: research questions that address issues faced by the study population and serve interests in improving their lives
- *Communication style*: an understanding of the preferred communication styles of the research participants and their communities and the subtleties and variations inherent in the language used
- *Awareness of identity and power differences*: a cognizance of researcher–participant power differences, the establishment of credibility, and the development of more horizontal relationships
- *Disclosure*: the avoidance of secrecy and the building of trust with the study population
- *Reciprocation*: research that meets mutual goals and objectives of the researcher and the study population
- *Empowerment*: a research process that contributes to empowering the study population
- *Time*: a flexible approach to time in the research process in terms of quantity and quality of time spent.

To these criteria I would add issues related specifically to linguistic diversity, taking into account the linguistic context of the respondents and the status of the respondents' language in relation to that of the researchers. All the research reported in this chapter took place in a context where English is the dominant language and, indeed, the only language used in the educational contexts of the research. Where the people researched belong to a linguistic minority the research should aim to empower them within the majority language population and there should be clear benefits for the researched that have been derived jointly by the researchers and researched.

Considering these criteria helps researchers to recognize that it is not only the methods employed but also the approach taken to development of the research questions and the subsequent analysis that need careful attention when researching with linguistic and cultural minorities. Culturally responsive research from social work, for example Casado *et al.* (2012), is useful for determining appropriate approaches. These authors argue that the incorporation of culturally responsive research practices with linguistic minorities has the potential to enhance trust and thus improve the recruitment and retention of linguistic minorities into programmes of research.

Our consideration of appropriate methodologies for research with cultural and linguistic minority populations can be enhanced by considering the work of psychology researchers, for example that of Lyons *et al.* (2012), who offer insight into considerations of qualitative research, particularly when working with people of African descent. The authors suggest that in such cases African cultural values such as holism and emphasis on relationships need to be taken into account at all stages of a research project, from topic selection and research team development to data analysis in order that the research may holistically and usefully represent the experiences of people of African descent. Researchers need to be similarly aware of the cultural values espoused by all respondents from minority populations when designing research.

In his discussions of education of linguistic minority children, Jim Cummins provides significant insights to other researchers. His model of 'intervention for collaborative empowerment' (2000: 45) enables discussion of appropriate approaches to schooling for linguistic and ethnic minority groups (see Figure 5.1). Cummins argues that the nature of macro-societal relations between dominant and minority groups influences the ways in which educational systems and educators themselves orient in daily interactions with those minority groups. He demonstrates how, if minority communities are subjected to dominance from educational institutions, their identity is subordinated. Therefore pedagogical choices about orientation towards such groups can act either to enable or disable minority groups' access to and opportunities in education. My work and research with linguistically and culturally diverse populations indicate that a similar approach could be taken to research. In the discussions that follow, I try to show how such collaboratively empowering research can be undertaken. Cummins is concerned with the interpersonal space that is constructed by the micro-interactions between students, educators and communities. Similarly the micro-interactions between researchers and researched create interpersonal spaces that give or deny voice and identity consolidation to the respondents.

Drawing from the four disciplines discussed and with the additions around language mentioned above these criteria will be referred to in the discussions of research projects in this chapter. The chapter ends with an account of how I have adapted Cummins's model and incorporated ideas from Meleis, Casado *et al.* and Lyons *et al.* to develop appropriate research methodologies when working with linguistically and ethnically diverse populations, and the resulting criteria for empowering educational research with linguistically and culturally diverse communities.

Coercive relation of power manifested in the macro-interaction between dominant group institutions and subordinated communities ⟶ Ambivalent/Insecure or resistant subordinated group identity

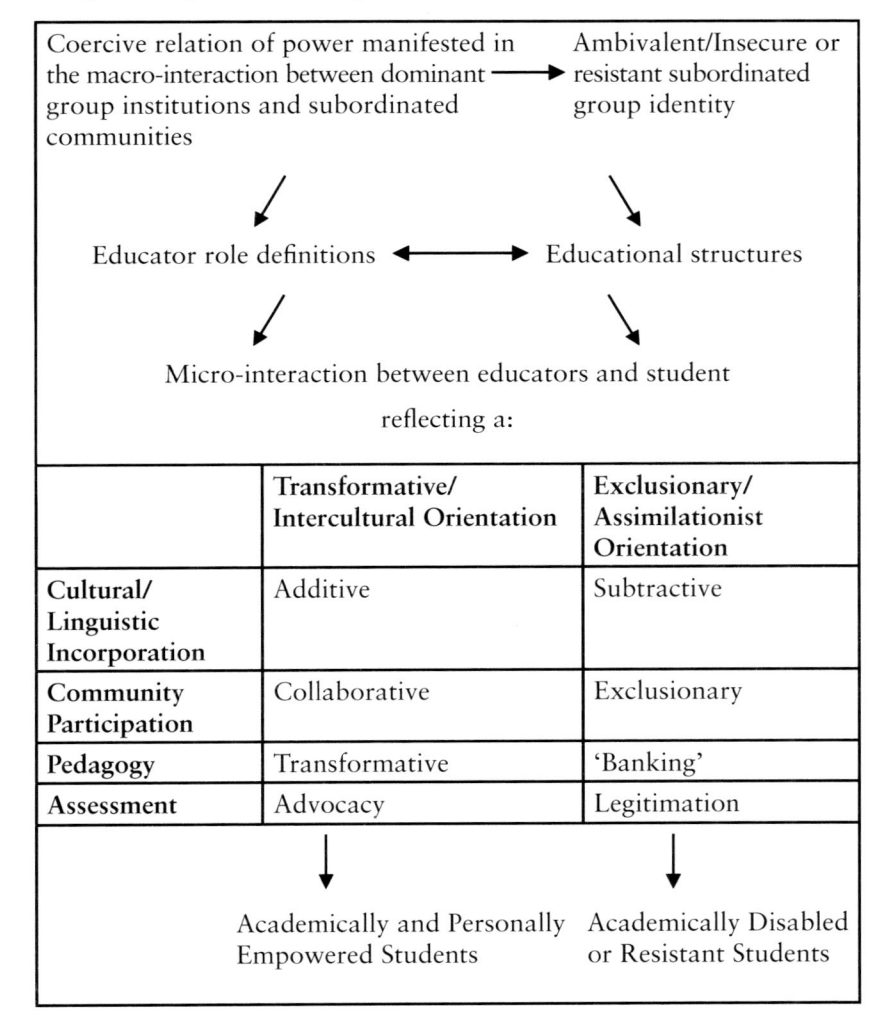

Educator role definitions ⟷ Educational structures

Micro-interaction between educators and student reflecting a:

	Transformative/ Intercultural Orientation	Exclusionary/ Assimilationist Orientation
Cultural/ Linguistic Incorporation	Additive	Subtractive
Community Participation	Collaborative	Exclusionary
Pedagogy	Transformative	'Banking'
Assessment	Advocacy	Legitimation

↓ Academically and Personally Empowered Students

↓ Academically Disabled or Resistant Students

Figure 5.1: Intervention for Collaborative Empowerment (Cummins, 2000: 45)

Geri Smyth

Contexts

Project 1: *Young people discuss diversity*

The first project was the 'Connections Conference for Children and Young People', part of a seminar series funded by the ESRC.[1] The Connections Conference gave young people the opportunity to discuss their views on Social Capital and Diversity. The 60 pupils attending the conference were between ten and 14 years old and came from three schools in Scotland. Their abilities and socioeconomic, linguistic and cultural backgrounds varied widely. We were keen to begin to understand young people's opinions and perspectives outwith the constraints of a classroom discussion where power relations within the school are likely to inhibit the student voices.

When organizing the event, the researchers (academics from three Scottish universities) tried to subvert the power differentials between adult researchers and young people who were positioned on the day as school pupils. We chose the venue carefully and decided on the MacRobert Playhouse[2] at the University of Stirling, which would be child-friendly. Venue is an important factor in accessing the voices of the less powerful, be this due to age or social status, and should make participants feel welcomed and unintimidated. The organizers consciously tried to underplay their own academic identities and the associated power and status, for instance wearing casual clothes and using first names.

The main part of the event used Open Space Technology,[3] which enables participants to determine their own agenda for discussion. We wanted the participants to be able to express their views confidently, knowing their views would be heard and respected and that the collaborative views generated through the research would promote greater understanding. The opening activity posed specific questions, stimulated by picture images from campaigns against discrimination, and invited the young people to consider who 'gets left out in school and out of school'. They were asked to comment on the messages contained in familiar television programmes and other cultural activities. They viewed the images in cross-school groups, and wrote their individual or collective thoughts on flipcharts. This enabled initial discussion, hopefully not inhibited by the presence of the adult researchers who were in the room but took no part in these discussions, or the accompanying teachers who sat quietly at the back of the room.

The researchers then led a whole group discussion based on the children's comments and posed a single question, '*How can we be more welcoming to others?*' Rather than inviting on the spot answers, the children were asked to write their responses on sticky notes and put them around the room. While the young people had refreshments the researchers grouped their sticky note responses around eight emerging themes, such as 'Racism', 'Sectarianism' and 'Respect'.[4] Discussion areas were established for each theme and the children were free to attend any of them for as long as they wished. Two rounds of discussions were held with no adult intervention and each discussion was audio recorded. The groups were told that the discussions would later be listened to by the adults and that they could turn off the recorders if they wished.

Once the conversations had been transcribed, they were collated into booklets, which were sent to the schools for distribution to all the participants, along with the images used on the day. Names were excluded from the transcriptions. We asked if the young people had anything they wished to add to or remove from the transcriptions but no one said they did.

Feedback during and after the event suggested that the young people had enjoyed the experience, particularly meeting and talking with pupils from other schools. They let us know that they had learned from the day but this notion of learning seemed to revert to the expected relationships between children and adults. Nonetheless the transcripts and recordings of the discussions did seem to suggest that participants were involved and engaged. The gathered data from the open space groupings was a set of unstructured, child-led discussions around issues of diversity, with between four and ten pupils participating in a group at any one time. The dialogue in Box 5.1 is an extract from a discussion on the theme of racism, intended as an example of the kind of data produced by this approach.

Pupil 1	*We're all the same except we're different.*
Pupil 2	*How does that work? We're not different at all.*
Pupil 3	*I mean, it's* [racism] *not just white people ganging up on coloured people, it can be coloured people ganging up on white people as well, no offence.* [This was said to a minority ethnic pupil in the group.]
Pupil 4	*I know.*
Pupil 3	*It's not as if you do it* [racism] *anyway.*

Box 5.1: Extract from pupil dialogue in the discussion group on racism

It appeared that the young people were uninhibited about how they talked around the issue of racism when no adults were present, and wished to negotiate meanings with each other. Conversations from the other themes showed similar negotiation of meaning, acceptance of different experiences and willingness to question one another's perspectives.

The intention was to allow for unstructured discussions, and to leave it to participants to take the topic in the direction of their choosing. However, we had not made this sufficiently clear to the accompanying teachers and some of them were unwilling or unable to relinquish their usual teacher positions of power, intervening in, controlling and steering the conversations. Even when teachers took no active part in the discussions, they asserted their power, intervening for instance, when they thought the pupils were too noisy. Clearly ways still need to be found for young people to talk freely with neither implicit nor explicit adult intervention.

The first consideration of the benefits and barriers of this approach to the research is whether or not the method overcame the power differential. The open space technology did allow a voice to the young people involved, but because we researchers were not present we could not tell who controlled the conversations. In relation to diversity in particular, elements of the conversations caused the researchers some discomfort, such as use of the term 'coloured people' (see Box 5.1). However this did signal the difficulties young people have when they discuss race without being clear about the terminology. The discussions appeared to enable the young people to draw on their own knowledge and experiences and it seemed that the outcomes were collaboratively built. The length and choice of topics for discussion were controlled by the participants themselves, allowing them greater agency than other methods. But we heard a lot of what we considered to be off-task talk, and could not tell if this related to the rest of the data around discrimination that we were interested in. The transcribed conversations suggested that the young people had forgotten about the recording and it sometimes became uncomfortably intrusive to read, as they veered towards adolescent jokes and personal comments about people not present.

It would have been useful to find ways of involving the young people in the analysis of the data, rather than merely inviting them to comment on the transcripts from a distance. Had we recalled the respondents to work with the transcriptions alongside us to generate categories we could have expanded the collaborative and transformative nature of the research.

Project 2: Investigating refugee pupils' creative responses to schooling

The second project is the EU-funded[5] project 'Creative Learning and Student Perspectives' (CLASP), which involved nine countries in local ethnographic projects. CLASP's overall aim was to identify how school pupils utilized their creativity to enable learning and to gain insight into pupils' perspectives on their own learning. The Scottish project focused on newly arrived migrant children who knew little English, in one Glasgow primary school. All had arrived in Glasgow as a result of the UK policy of dispersing asylum seekers and thus faced multiple and intersecting layers of minority status, as they were not only cultural, ethnic and linguistic minorities but also newly arrived asylum seekers. The Scottish project sought to identify the creative strategies used by the young children from asylum-seeking families to access learning and a curriculum in a new language and educational system, and the discussion here refers to one part of a long-term ethnographic project.

Accessing pupil perspectives can be problematic when there is no common language, so the pupils were given digital cameras and shown how to use them to record their perspectives on learning and the school environment. Pupils aged 8–12 years worked in teams of four 'co-researchers' – two from asylum-seeking families and two pupils who were long-term in the school and who spoke English as their first language, with one camera per team. The researcher gave the pupils basic instructions for use of the camera and asked each group to take photos of whatever or whoever interested them in the school context. The researcher then helped the pupils to develop the skills to manipulate the photographs and to create annotated slide shows.

The resultant data for this part of the project were a set of slideshows derived from pupils' photographs (see the photo and comment in Figure 5.2). Many of the photographs showed people but for reasons of confidentiality the example here does not include pupils or teachers in the school. The photo and comment in Figure 5.2 are by a 10-year-old boy recently arrived from Algeria. His home language is Arabic and he is commenting on how seeing the Arabic words for 'welcome' on the poster helped him to feel he belonged in the school.

Geri Smyth

Figure 5.2: Extract of annotated pupil slideshow

The young people in this project had control over the topic, the interpretation and the dissemination of their views. They chose which photos to annotate and share with the researcher to make up the data set, and the comments were clearly the pupils' interpretation and not one imposed by adults. However, as mentioned in relation to Project 1, some teachers were unwilling to fully hand over control to the pupils, decided when the cameras could be used, and wanted to see the photos before the pupils had organized their data. The collaboration between pupils nonetheless helped skills development and also fostered a two-way integration of the new pupils into the school.

Consequently all the pupils became both academically and personally empowered through their engagement in the project.

Project 3: Discussing refugee teachers' experiences

The third approach emanates from the 'Refugees Into Teaching in Scotland' (RITeS) project funded by the Scottish Government between 2006 and 2011. The project wished to understand the routes to re-professionalization of teachers who wished to rejoin the teaching profession in their new land, having been forced to flee their country and seek asylum in the UK. These refugee teachers were extremely diverse in their ethnicity, language, religion and residence status. It was decided that as the group themselves were intimately interested in the findings of the research, they should be intimately involved in the shaping of the research. A working group of researchers, respondents, stakeholders, including the Scottish Refugee Council and the General Teaching Council for Scotland, was accordingly set up to co-construct the research tools and jointly analyse the data gathered from in-depth semi-structured interviews. The key researcher in the project, a refugee himself who had been a teacher in his country of origin, was fluent in both French and English and conducted interviews in either language according to the respondent's preference. The French language interviews were transcribed in French and also translated into English.

Continued discussion of the tools to be used resulted in an interview schedule that got to the heart of the issues facing the respondents. The ongoing involvement of the researched with the process, and the openness of the researcher in discussing his own journey to re-employment, won the respondents' trust, and they appreciated the value of the research. This justified the time taken to construct the interview schedule because it was co-constructed by the entire working group. The analysis was similarly discussed by the working group, although this compromised the clarity about which data could be validly recognized as research data to be analysed (see below). The personal approach to data collection evoked comments that demonstrated that the respondents had both agency in the process and ownership of the generated data, an example of which is provided in Box 5.2.

However, although the analysis of the data was enriched by the involvement of those interviewed, it caused *post hoc* data to be uncovered as the respondents discussed the transcripts and it was difficult to know when participation ceased.

> I want to get back into the profession I love. I would like to do something to keep my mind occupied in the teaching profession.
>
> Male, DR Congo (Kinshasa), Secondary
>
> I am a teacher. I want to remain a teacher. I haven't done any other thing outside teaching. I don't see myself doing anything else apart from teaching.
>
> Male, Congo (Brazzaville), Secondary

Box 5.2: Extract of interview data from participatory research with refugee teachers

Discussion

I now return to the criteria itemized earlier in the chapter and Cummins's model to discuss how the three contexts here were informed by these approaches. Attempting to research valid perceptions of the attitudes to and experiences of diversity can be problematic. It is particularly difficult to ascertain the opinions of pupils towards diversity among their school peers because the context of the school curriculum and policies and equality legislation may influence what they believe can be said when adults are listening. When those adults are the teachers who generally set the parameters of discussion, barriers to accessing validated opinions are almost inevitable. The interpersonal space already established between the pupils and adults in coercive relations of power is unlikely to promote open discussion of issues that may be controversial. Open Space was supportive in offering a more collaborative interpersonal space than school but we cannot claim that what was said was not inhibited by the presence of teachers and other adults. Although there was much off-task talk in the recordings, the transcriptions offered important insights into pupils' conversation when they were feeling rather less inhibited.

While the agenda for discussion was set by the young people themselves, the adult researchers set the scene and provided the prompts that led to the agenda. This was essential to achieve a discussion around diversity and did not detract from the openness of the resultant dialogues. Rather, enabling the formation of discussion groups around areas of interest specified by the young people themselves led to less structured and more open conversations than would have been possible with, for example, focus groups. The absence of adults limited attempts by pupils to take over or dominate conversations in order to impress. Evidence from the transcripts demonstrated the pupils' respect for each other's opinions. It remains difficult to know however whether or not the young people completely understood the nature of how the discussions might be considered, despite our best efforts to achieve informed assent to participation. It is also difficult to assess whether this mode of research enabled linguistic minority pupils to participate more fully than alternative methods may have allowed. The discussions were all in English but room did appear to be made for all to contribute and respect for personal experience was apparent. Although the design of the project purposely gave space to the young people and they determined the agenda for discussion, the research did not meet all of Meleis's criteria, specifically as regards context, communication style and time. As researchers, we were not totally familiar with the context of the young people chosen by their schools to participate. We intended that the adult-free conversations would enable meaningful communication but audio recording of conversations is not necessarily familiar to young people. Time was a major constraint in this project, as we only had one day with the young people and no time was allowed for reflection, or for their involvement in analysis of the data.

The second project however was purposely designed to enable the participation of linguistic minority pupils and to empower them to contribute. The participants in this research were very keen to progress in school but were at first hindered by their limited access to classroom English. The researcher wished to ascertain the creative approaches utilized by these pupils to access the new curriculum, language and education system. The local authority required that the opportunities be delivered to both the newly arrived and the established pupils. The teams of young researchers that were set up enabled all the children to participate and share their skills and knowledge. The project design addressed all of Meleis's criteria and took full account of the call for culturally responsive methodologies highlighted by Casado *et al.* and Lyons *et al.* The context of the newly arrived pupils from asylum-seeking families grappling with a new home and educational environment in a new language was at the heart of the research design, which focused on generating friendships and building on the respondents' experiences. The young people themselves helped to generate the research questions as they strove to make sense of the new surroundings. The use of digital photography overcame communication difficulties between children who spoke different languages and the pupil research groups worked alongside the researcher to make sense of the data. The study took place over 18 months and this allowed relationships to grow. The pupils had control over which photos were revealed to the researcher for joint analysis.

None of the children were familiar with photographic software, so the researcher was able to teach new skills to all of them. The children chose the topics for the photos they would present to the researcher, and determined how these would be manipulated and annotated in advance of presentation. Thus the respondents were given power and control and were not limited by a poor command of English. Ethical approval for the project required that the children were restricted to taking photos only inside the school and its grounds but this was insignificant since the focus of the research was on how the new arrivals were responding to school in Scotland and the data collected by the pupils gave a clear picture of what and who was meaningful in the negotiation of their new context. The respondents' annotations captured the meanings of their photographs and assisted in the analysis of the data. The groups of four each presented their photo show and the researcher recorded the narrative of their discussions, which made clear who had contributed what to the task. The process gave the respondents opportunities to develop their thoughts before letting the researcher know what they wished to say and enhanced their understanding of the nature of the research. This is particularly important when the researcher and the researched do not have a common language. By creating artefacts there was material that could be returned to later in the ethnographic research. The artefacts were also valued by the participants, as were the certificates of participation designed and given out by the researcher.

Refugees are subjected to considerable research but receive little immediate beneficial outcome. Both the tangible recognition of participation and the new skills these participants developed helped to overcome the researcher's concerns about the perceived value of the research for the respondents. The researched were empowered through all aspects of the project's design.

The third project discussed in this chapter involved adult participants, all from linguistic and ethnic minorities and all refugees who had fled from their country of origin where they had been educational professionals, mostly teachers. These were ideal respondents for a research project seeking insights into the re-professionalization of refugee teachers, so it was fitting that they be involved in the creation of the research tools and the data analysis. A small team of researchers was created, made up of two refugee teachers, two academics and two stakeholders, one from the local authority and one from the professional accreditation body. The group met regularly to discuss approaches to the research and to develop the semi-structured interview schedule. Some initial concerns of the academics and stakeholders about what could be seen as intrusive questioning with potentially vulnerable informants were dealt with in the discussions with the refugee teachers. The sharing of the analysis led to greater insights than if the data been considered only by 'outsider' academics. A discussion on the use of idioms generated valuable analysis about the difficulties re-professionalization presented. This co-constructed analysis was made possible by the high professional and academic backgrounds of all the members of the group. Such co-analysis of data may not be as straightforward if attempted with younger school pupils or with respondents with less educational capital.

Returning to Cummins's model of collaborative empowerment, it seems that some research may be characterized by the domination of minority groups by powerful majority group researchers with a particular agenda and little concern for the impact of their research on those researched. If researchers pay little attention to the cultural and linguistic identities of the researched they are likely to evoke ambivalence or even resistance to the research. Alternatively, methodologies can be co-constructed to ensure that the research is transformative for those participating, affording them new skills and knowledge.

Research design choices when working with linguistic and cultural minority groups must act to enable their access to and investment in the research. Institutional and national ethical guidelines for the conduct of research should embed the development of collaborative relations of power between researcher and researched. In this way the criteria suggested from the range of disciplines that undertake research with minority communities can be incorporated to offer guidelines for the design of such research in education as illustrated in Figure 5.3.

This chapter aims to help researchers working in educational contexts with cultural and linguistic minorities to design research that will overcome some potential pitfalls and will both empower the respondents and yield valid and purposeful data.

```
┌─────────────────────────────────────────────────────────────────────────┐
│ Collaborative relations of power (construction)    Empowered, confident and │
│ manifested in the macro-interactions between  →   articulated minority group │
│ majority group research institution and minority   identity              │
│ group communities                                                        │
│                    ↙                        ↘                            │
│         Researcher role definitions  ←→  Research structures             │
│                    ↘                        ↙                            │
│         Micro-interactions between researchers and researched reflecting a │
│              Transformative/Intercultural Orientation                    │
└─────────────────────────────────────────────────────────────────────────┘
```

Cultural/Linguistic Incorporation Relevance of research questions and preferred communication style and language of respondents carefully considered at design stage. Cultural and linguistic diversity recognized as offering added value to the data and the analysis.

Community Participation Collaborative, horizontal relationships developed between researchers and respondents with the adoption through co-construction of tools, of culturally responsive methodologies.

Methodology Culturally responsive, creative and transformative methodological approaches that empower participants, offering access to new skills that build on own knowledge and experiential base.

Analysis Time taken to ensure that the initial relevance of questions is continued into the analysis and reporting of data in a way that advocates by and for minority communities rather than acting to legitimize failure.

↓

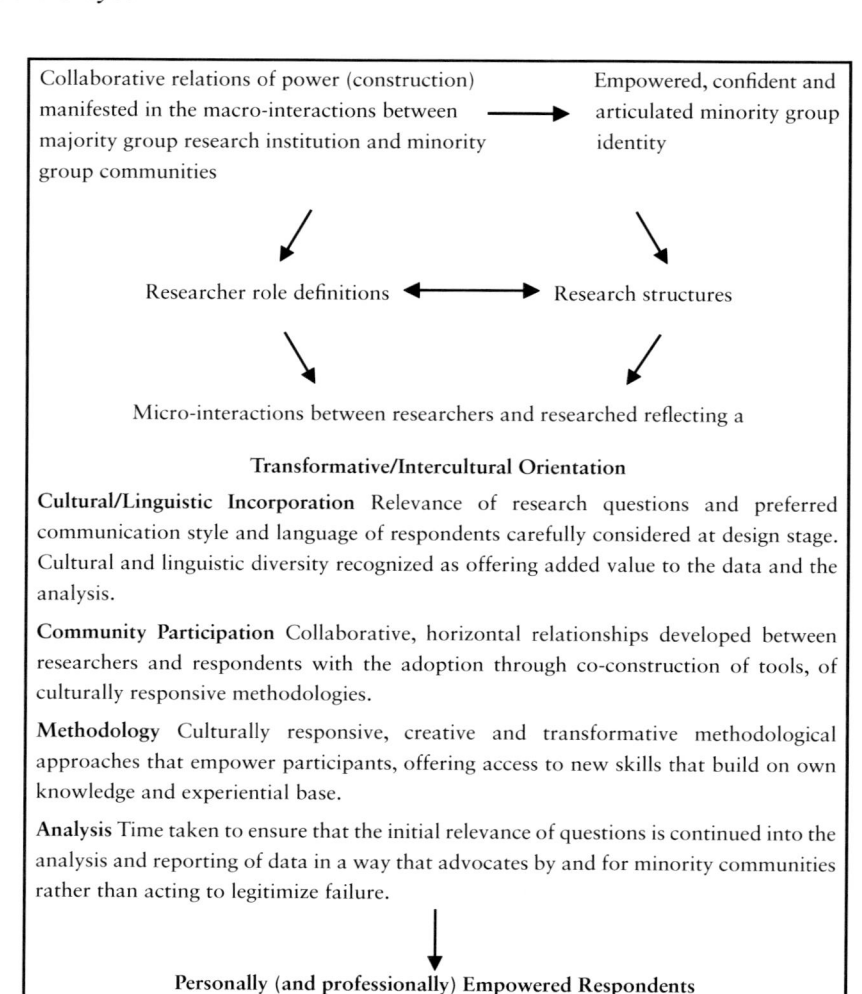

Personally (and professionally) Empowered Respondents

Figure 5.3: Collaborative empowerment through research (Smyth, adapted from Cummins, 2000)

References

Allan, J., Smyth, G., I'Anson, J. and Mott, J. (2009) 'Understanding disability with children's social capital'. *Journal of Research in Special Educational Needs*, 9 (2), 115–21.

Casado, B.L., Negi, N.J. and Hong, M. (2012) 'Culturally competent social work research: Methodological considerations for research with language minorities'. *Social Work*, 57 (1), 1–10.

Cummins, J. (2000) *Language, Power, and Pedagogy: Bilingual children in the crossfire*. Clevedon, UK, and Buffalo, NY: Multilingual Matters.

Kum, H., Menter, I. and Smyth, G. (2008) *Refugees into Teaching in Scotland Research Project*. Online. www.strath.ac.uk/media/departments/childhoodandprimarystudies/rites/ritesresearchprojectreport/Final_Report_Dec_08.pdf (accessed May 2014).

Lyons, H.Z., Bike, D.H., Johnson, A. and Bethea, A. (2012) 'Culturally competent qualitative research with people of African descent'. *Journal of Black Psychology*, 38 (2), 153–71.

Meleis, A.I. (1996) 'Culturally competent scholarship: Substance and rigor'. *Advances in Nursing Science*, 19 (2), 1–16.

Smyth, G. (2006) 'Multilingual conferencing: Effective teaching of children from refugee and asylum-seeking families'. *Improving Schools*, 9 (2), 99–109.

Endnotes

[1] Economic and Social Research Council (ESRC) seminar series, *Social Capital, Professionalism, and Diversity* (RES–451–25–4012).

[2] www.macrobert.org/playhouse.htm

[3] www.openspaceworld.org

[4] The other five themes were 'How We Might Get On Better'; 'Disability'; 'Sexism'; 'Bullying'; and 'What Happens Outside School'.

[5] A European Commission funded project through the Socrates programme 6.1 Number 2002–4682/002–001 SO2–610 BGE.

Chapter 6

Researcher as cartographer: Mapping the experiences of culturally diverse research participants
Ninetta Santoro

Research in culturally diverse education contexts presents particular difficulties for researchers who are outsiders to the communities they investigate. Designing research that is culturally sensitive, establishing relationships of trust with participants with whom researchers do not share cultural practices and values, and effectively gaining access to research sites, is imperative for researchers who seek to understand the perspectives, identities and social relationships of the cultural Other. Of particular significance is the need for researchers to understand how their own encultured positionings shape the research process, from the formation of a research question to the research design, the data collection and the data analysis. Clarke points to the researcher's positioning in shaping the research direction:

> Beginning even before a research topic is decided upon, we notice and store information, impressions, and images about topic areas and issues. Not only are there are no *tabula rasa* researchers, but we also come with a lot of baggage. Such ideas and preconceptions become intellectual wallpaper of sorts, background tacit assumptions sometimes operating as it were, behind our backs in the research process.
>
> (Clarke, 2005: 85)

Much qualitative educational research is about the telling of stories by participants through interviews, and sometimes practice, and the retelling of those stories by researchers. 'The way in which we produce stories is undeniably influenced by our own gaze, our standpoint, the history we bring to a research moment' (Nelson and Gould, 2005: 329). Researchers need to be reflexive, to constantly interrogate their own assumptions about

Researcher as cartographer

what it is they take for granted, what they listen for and how they hear what they are told.

In this chapter I discuss the method of analysis I adopted for the examination of longitudinal interview data from a case study that investigated the experiences and career pathways of newly graduated Indigenous[1] teachers in Australian schools over a three-year period, from 2005 to 2008. This longitudinal case study is a component of a larger study that brought together a team of Indigenous and non-Indigenous researchers to interview 54 teachers, both current and former, newly graduated and experienced, across regional and rural Australia (for details of the study, see Santoro *et al.*, 2011; Santoro, 2010; Reid *et al.*, 2009). The imperative for the research was the need to understand why Indigenous people are under-represented in the teaching profession in Australia despite calls for an increase in their numbers that began more than thirty years ago (Hughes and Willmot, 1982).

In the instance of the longitudinal case study reported here, researchers conducted semi-structured interview conversations with four newly graduated teachers, twice a year for three years. A longitudinal approach enabled the researchers to explore the complexities of the interviewees' experiences over an extended period of time, to see continuities and discontinuities with regards to how they experienced their work. The interviewees, guided by open-ended questions, narrated aspects of their lives and engaged in storytelling that produced rich 'first-order narratives' (Elliot, 2005: 12). The questions aimed to elicit chronological, experiential accounts of their schooling, their family backgrounds, their pre-service teacher education, their induction into teaching and their experiences as new professionals, including the nature of their pedagogies, their relationships with students, parents and colleagues, and their professional challenges, successes and disappointments. During each interview, the interviewees' attention was drawn to particular recounted events, experiences and perceptions and they were then asked to reflect on them. The data collected from each participant over time became an increasingly complex assembly of intersecting, complementary and/or conflicting vignettes of experience that would 'build over the course of several interviews and traverse temporal and geographical space' (Reissman, 2008: 23).

On reading and re-reading the interview transcripts, it became apparent to the researchers that the new graduates' professional experiences were complex and changing, and shaped by a myriad of human and non-human factors such as relationships with colleagues, their location in rural areas, Indigenous cultures, teacher recruitment policies and practices and so on. The researchers were interested in exploring not only the events and discourses that shaped the new graduates' transitions to teaching and their early teaching experiences, but also the ways in which these events were understood differently over the three-year period. Certain events took greater prominence at various times and diminished in importance at other times. These changing events contributed to the construction of fluid, changeable and postmodern teaching identities that were characterized by 'partialities, positionalities, complications, tenuousness, instabilities, irregularities, contradictions, heterogeneities, situatedness, and fragmentation – complexities' (Clarke, 2005: xxiv).

Some of the factors shaping the participants' lives were totally outside my realm of experience and were foreign to me as a non-Indigenous middle-class academic. I, like many researchers who choose to work in culturally diverse contexts, was faced with the challenge of trying to understand a context to which I was, essentially, an outsider. While I am not interested in achieving an accurate or a truthful reading of data, because there is never only one reality or truth nor just one way of understanding the world, I am interested in understanding my participants' viewpoints and perspectives, (as far as this can be possible). White middle-class researchers, Nelson and Gould ask of themselves and their work with marginalized women of colour, 'What can't we see in our research transcripts? ... When we interpret another person's words, what is important to think about? Perhaps most importantly, how can we be aware of what we don't know?' (2005: 332). In trying to make sense of the data before me, I was acutely aware that there were likely to be a number of nuances and complexities about the context under investigation that I might miss in my reading of the data because of my particular enculturated position. How could I come to know these complexities and make them visible? Haggis asserts 'We need to find ways of standing outside of our histories, circumstances and fields, and of examining our epistemological and ontological assumptions' (2009: 389). Den Outer *et al.*, commenting on this claim, suggest that:

> Although it is questionable to what extent it is possible to stand 'outside our histories, circumstances and fields', we argue that a way of knowing differently is achieved by revisiting our research methods and analytical approaches. What would improve the tool kit of the education researcher to enhance reflexive practice, and thus address those epistemological and ontological assumptions as a matter of course?
>
> (den Outer *et al.*, 2012: 1)

'Situational analysis', a framework developed by Adele Clarke, and an extension of grounded theory, was useful to me in understanding the complexities of the context or situation under investigation because it seeks to 'analyse a particular situation of interest through the specification, re-representation, and subsequent examinations of the most salient elements in that situation and their relations' (Clarke, 2005: 29). These salient elements are made visible through a series of maps that enable the researcher to see them in relation to each other and in relation to larger social worlds beyond the specific and immediate context under investigation.

In this chapter, I describe the process of constructing maps out of the data from the six interviews I conducted with Luke, one of the newly graduated teachers in the study described above. Luke is a Wiradjuri[2] man who was motivated to become a teacher because of his desire to help Indigenous people (the most socially and educationally disadvantaged group in Australia) improve their education outcomes. His first two teaching positions after graduation were at secondary schools where there were significant numbers of Indigenous students. In his third year of teaching, Luke moved to a school where there were no Indigenous students. I was interested in understanding the factors that had shaped this decision. Why did he move to a school where there were no Indigenous students after having been deeply involved in Indigenous education for the first two years of his career?

Situational analysis: Making maps from data

Situational analysis is what Khaw calls 'an analytic diagramming tool' (2012: 138) because it involves the researcher producing through drawing, a series of maps that make the 'invisible and inchoate social features of the situation more visible' (Clarke, 2005: 572). Maps 'create a visual representation of complexity. They open up the "knowledge space" in the way that they can hold multiplicity, heterogeneity and "messiness"' (den Outer *et al.*, 2012: 4). The maps constructed in situational analysis take account of the human and non-human elements in the particular situation under investigation. The human elements are key individuals or key groups of individuals who play a significant part in a situation, or political or economic elements, or temporal elements, for example, historical elements that are significant in a situation. The non-human elements of a particular situation can be technologies, infrastructures, 'things' such as sociocultural/symbolic elements such as religion, or spatial elements, such as geography.

Situational analysis, as originally conceived by Clarke, involves the production of three types of maps: situational maps (both 'messy' and 'relational'), 'social worlds/arenas maps' and 'positional maps'. Situational maps are macro-level maps that depict the major aspects or elements in a situation. There are two types of these maps: messy maps and relational maps. The second type of map is a meso-level map: a social worlds/arenas map that depicts the social worlds that constitute the situation under study. The third type of map, positional maps, is a micro-level map that is concerned with the 'major positions *taken in the data* on major discursive issues' (Clarke, 2005: 126). Like a growing body of researchers across a wide range of disciplines (Mills *et al.*, 2008; Llewellyn and Northway, 2007; Khaw, 2012), I have chosen to take from Clarke's framework what is appropriate and useful to my research focus. I have therefore constructed situational maps, both messy maps and relational maps, and a social worlds/arenas map. These maps are of the greatest use in understanding the context under investigation. As I read and re-read the interview transcripts, I asked of the data, 'Who and what are in this situation? Who and what matters in this situation? What elements "make a difference" in this situation?' (Clarke, 2005: 87). While the situation I was exploring was Luke's professional life, it became apparent that the boundaries between the personal and the professional were not clear.

Making messy situational maps

After I had read each interview text, I drew messy situational maps that contained human and non-human factors important to the situation. These included geographical locations, significant people, policies, teaching practices and so on. Each map is a 'a preliminary map that roughly lays out all the elements you (the researcher) think may be in that situation' (Clarke, 2005: 267). The various elements were placed randomly and without concern for their positioning on the page, although I positioned 'Luke' roughly in the centre. In the interest of optimising space in this chapter, I have combined the elements of interviews one and two in each year of the longitudinal study and presented them within the one situational map, although, originally, I drew a situational map for each interview. Each of the maps that follows is accompanied by a biographical narrative constructed from the multitude of smaller narratives Luke told me during the course of our interview, and from the mapped elements.

Researcher as cartographer

```
volunteer at community
        centre        high Indigenous population    physical education coordinator  taught only Indigenous students  low achieving students
                              new graduate
                                                      Tracey's good job
    physical education teacher
                         first in family to get degree   recruitment of Indigenous teachers
                                              Luke
              working class family   non-Indigenous girlfriend                              role model      transfer to Sydney
                       Crossthwaite High School
              taught life skills      committed to Indigenous education
                                           modified                   sports coach
         established AECG branch      curriculum   advised colleagues
                                    liaised with students' families      excursions and camps
              separate classes for Indigenous
                         students                 cultural expert
                                                                          committee chair     footballer
              mentor  out-of-school programme
                                     difficult but rewarding teaching                 Tracey and Luke engaged
              boys-only class          only Indigenous teacher in school
              Bachelor of Teaching             teaching position in country
                                                          school
```

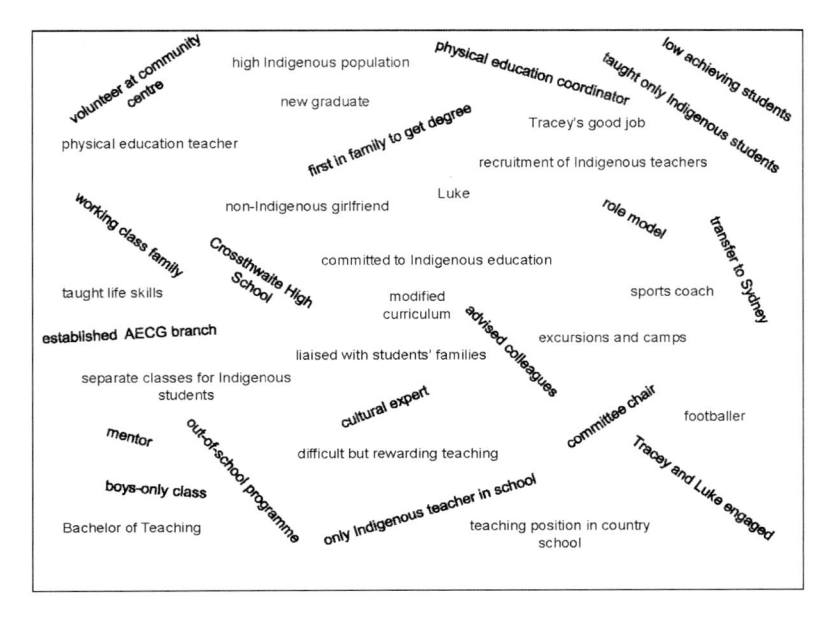

Figure 6.1: Messy situational map: Year one

Luke grew up in a small town of approximately 5,000 people located several hundreds of kilometres from Sydney. His father was brought up on a nearby church mission and had limited formal education, having left school at the age of ten. His mother's family were farm workers and she too, had limited formal education. Luke, the youngest of their three children, attended the local government primary and secondary school where the student population was about 80 per cent Indigenous. He was a good sportsman, and in particular, a good footballer. After he finished secondary school he moved to Sydney to play with a major football team for three years. His girlfriend Tracey, who is not Indigenous, went with him. Although he enjoyed playing semi-professional football and was mostly successful, a number of injuries prompted him to look elsewhere for a long-term career. He had always wanted to be a physical education teacher and he thought it would enable him to do something he loved, would provide a secure and stable income and enable him to help other Indigenous people. When he was 21, he responded to calls to recruit Indigenous people into teaching and enrolled in a Bachelor of Teaching, specializing in Health and Physical Education. He was one of the few in his family to complete secondary school and the first to obtain a university education. While he was studying, he volunteered to develop and conduct, in his spare time, special out-of-school programmes for Indigenous children at a local community centre, including cultural programmes and a programme about careers in sport.

Luke's first position after graduating was an ongoing permanent position at a secondary school in a small country town not far from Sydney, Crossthwaite High School. The school had a population of Indigenous students, but he was the only Indigenous teacher. He was given a Year 9 (aged 14 to 15 years) boys-only class, a group consisting of 15 students, most of whom were Indigenous. They had low academic outcomes and significant social problems. The principal thought that having all the students in the one class would enable the teachers to address their needs more effectively. The class was considered by the staff to be the most challenging in the school. Luke modified the curriculum for the students, took them on excursions and camps, taught them life skills, taught them about Indigenous culture, played sport with them at lunchtime and visited their families. He enjoyed his work and found the contact with the boys difficult, but rewarding. He planned for the National Indigenous and Islander Day of Celebrations (NAIDOC), helped establish a branch of the Aboriginal Education Consultative Group (AECG) in the region, and a few weeks after he began at the school, became the Physical Education coordinator.

In November of the same year, Tracey accepted a job in Sydney that was too good to turn down because of the high salary and the apartment (in a desirable area of Sydney) that her employer offered. Although he loved Crossthwaite High and would have liked to have stayed, Luke asked the Department of Education to be transferred to Sydney the following year. He was prepared to go to any school in Sydney that was within reasonable travelling time from his home if it had Indigenous students because he wanted to use his skills and knowledge to help his own people. However, there were no ongoing positions available, so Luke took leave of absence and put his name on a central list of teachers who were available the following year for casual relief teaching. Luke and Tracey got engaged in December that year.

In January, Luke was offered relief teaching at Boundary High. It had a high proportion of Indigenous students. When the principal found out Luke was Indigenous, he asked him to run a special programme three days a week for a small withdrawal class of Year 8 Indigenous boys with social and academic problems. Luke was keen to help. He modified curriculum materials across all disciplines, taught the boys life skills, organized guest speakers, ran anger management sessions, tried to develop the boys' pride

Researcher as cartographer

in their Indigeneity, counselled and mentored them. He also team-taught with colleagues in a support role and helped them understand the needs of Indigenous students. It was challenging and hard work and he had to physically intervene in fights between students on many occasions. For the other two days of the week he took classes in any subject area for teachers who were on leave. Sometimes they left a programme for him to follow; sometimes they did not.

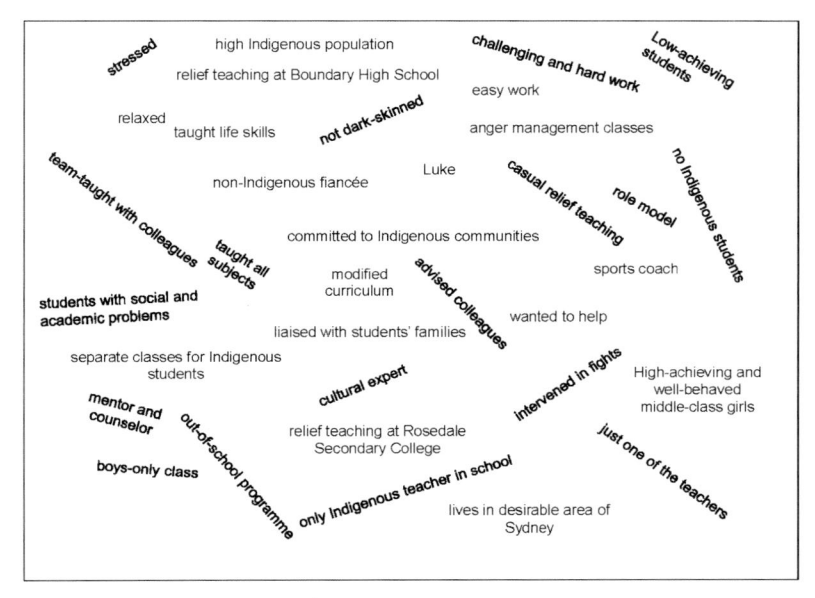

A "messy situational map" diagram containing the following terms arranged around the name "Luke" in the center: stressed; high Indigenous population; relief teaching at Boundary High School; challenging and hard work; Low-achieving students; relaxed; easy work; taught life skills; not dark-skinned; anger management classes; team-taught with colleagues; non-Indigenous fiancée; casual relief teaching; role model; no Indigenous students; committed to Indigenous communities; taught all subjects; modified curriculum; advised colleagues; sports coach; students with social and academic problems; liaised with students' families; wanted to help; separate classes for Indigenous students; cultural expert; intervened in fights; High-achieving and well-behaved middle-class girls; mentor and counsellor; out-of-school programme; relief teaching at Rosedale Secondary College; just one of the teachers; boys-only class; only Indigenous teacher in school; lives in desirable area of Sydney.

Figure 6.2: Messy situational map: Year two

In October, after having registered his interest for relief teaching at another school, Rosedale Secondary College, a short distance from home, he was contacted and asked to work two days of the week, every week. He continued part-time with the boys' programme at Boundary High but went to Rosedale Secondary College for the remainder of the week. In comparison to Boundary High, his work there was easy. It was a non-government middle-class girls' school, the academic standards were high, discipline problems were non-existent, the girls always brought pens and paper to class and there were never any fights in class. The regular teachers always left Luke a programme to follow when he filled in for them while they took leave. Tracey commented on him being less tired and less stressed when he came home from school on the two days he was at Rosedale.

There were no Indigenous students at Rosedale and no one knew Luke was Indigenous. He did not tell anyone. While Luke is not fair-skinned, he is not very dark, nor does he have stereotypical Indigenous features.

81

Ninetta Santoro

People who do not know him well do not assume he is Indigenous. In his own words, at Rosedale he was 'just one of the teachers'.

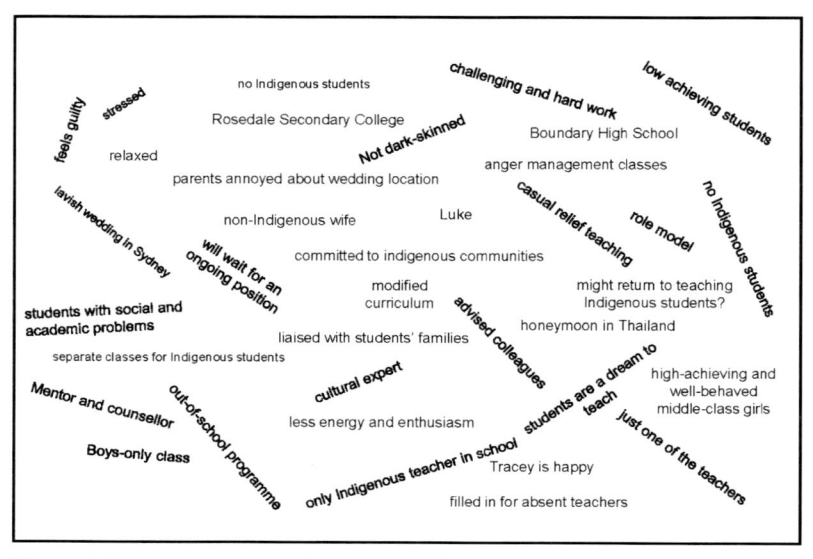

Figure 6.3: Messy situational map: Year three

During the January of Luke's second year of teaching, he and Tracey were married in lavish style in Sydney. To their parents' annoyance, they decided not to have their wedding in their hometown because there was nowhere nice to have the reception. Their family and friends all travelled down to Sydney. They had their honeymoon in Thailand before Luke started back at Boundary High to run similar programmes to those he had conducted the year before. But he still did not have an ongoing permanent position. The Year 9 boys were now in Year 10 and there was a new cohort of Year 9 boys that had taken their place. They had similar problems as the students from the previous year. Luke worked with them in the same ways as he had with the others, but he felt his energy and enthusiasm waning. In September, the staffing coordinator at Rosedale High offered him work for the rest of the school year covering for a teacher who was on maternity leave. He decided to accept it. He says teaching is a lot easier there than at Boundary. The girls are 'a dream' to teach. Tracey thinks it was the best decision he has made.

Luke hopes that an ongoing permanent position will become available at Rosedale next year. But even if it does not, he will stay on as a relief teacher and wait for something to come up. He enjoys working there a lot. But he says he feels guilty. He also says he will go back to teaching Indigenous students – one day.

Making relational maps

The next step I took was to construct a relational map of each messy map. This involved drawing lines between elements to show their connection. The end result of the linking of various elements was a mass of converging lines connecting some elements with others. In what follows, I present relational maps for each of the three years.

In the relational map for year one (Figure 6.4), there are clusters of connecting lines around a number of key elements: 'commitment to Indigenous education'; 'Crossthwaite High School'; the 'only Indigenous teacher' and the 'need for Indigenous teachers'. As part of the analysis process, I considered these clusters, teasing out the complexities of each, and thinking about them in relation to the other clusters of relational lines. Firstly, 'need for Indigenous teachers' is a socio-political element of the context under study. As mentioned earlier, Indigenous teachers are under-represented in the profession and there have been ongoing calls to increase their numbers. Luke responded to such calls by applying for entry to teacher education via the special entry opportunities that had been put in place by universities. Therefore, he was appointed after graduation to a school with a population of Indigenous students. In this school, Luke was able to put into practice his knowledge about Indigenous students, their cultural practices and their educational needs. His 'commitment to Indigenous education' reflected his own biography and life experiences as an Indigenous person and was realized by him taking on a huge range of responsibilities, including acting as a cultural expert and as a bridge between Indigenous and school communities. He was a role model for Indigenous students, actively involved in the pastoral care of Indigenous students and responsible for the implementation of Indigenous education strategies, extra-curricular activities, such as camps and anger management workshops and the coaching of sports teams after school and at the weekend. He sat on school committees and external committees concerned with Indigenous education and often took on the role of adviser to his non-Indigenous colleagues who looked to him for advice about pedagogies that would be likely to be successful with Indigenous students. That he was the 'only Indigenous teacher at the school' meant that this range of responsibilities fell to him, even though he was a beginning and inexperienced teacher.

Ninetta Santoro

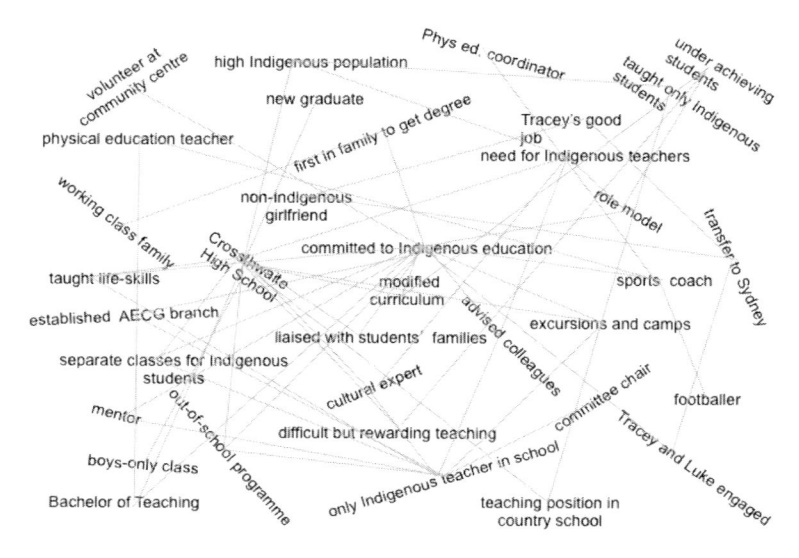

Figure 6.4: Relational map: Year one

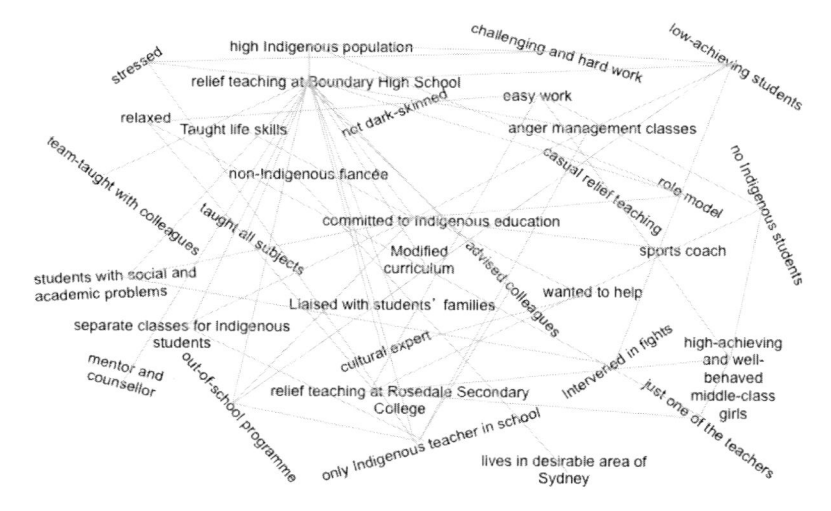

Figure 6.5: Relational map: Year two

The connecting lines in the second relational map converge at similar points as was the case in the first map, that is, 'commitment to Indigenous education' and 'only Indigenous teacher in school'. 'Boundary High School', 'Rosedale Secondary College' and 'high-achieving middle-class girls' have also emerged as elements where clusters of relational lines converge. Rosedale, while still only offering Luke casual relief teaching, was a less stressful workplace where he did not need to work after the school day had ended and he did not need to take responsibility single-handedly for Indigenous education. Luke was able to be 'just a teacher' at Rosedale rather than 'an Indigenous teacher'. In the absence of information about his cultural background, his colleagues at Rosedale did not assume him to be Indigenous.

The relational map for year three (Figure 6.6) looks quite different from the previous relational maps. The clusters of relational lines converging at different points indicate a shift in importance in human and non-human factors. 'Rosedale Secondary College' has emerged as a significant factor (especially in the second half of the year). Previously, 'low-achieving students' had been a major factor in Luke's professional work, as were all of the additional responsibilities he took on. However, these demands and challenges have become less important than other factors such as 'high-achieving and well-behaved middle-class girls', 'easy work', being 'relaxed' and 'Tracey is happy'. Of significance is Luke's changing lifestyle, which is evident in such elements as a 'lavish wedding in Sydney', rather than in his hometown, and a 'honeymoon in Thailand'. Luke's reported feelings of guilt and his claim that he 'might to go back to teaching Indigenous kids – one day', cannot be ignored and suggests a degree of ambivalence about his decision to take up a position at Rosedale.

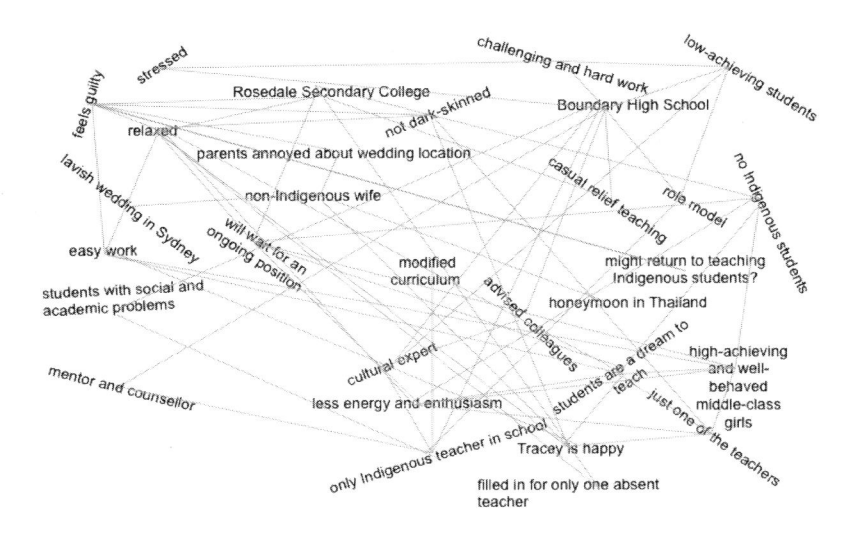

Figure 6.6: Relational map: Year three

Making social worlds/arenas maps

In constructing the social worlds/arenas map, I looked for the significant elements that emerged out of the relational maps and considered how they constitute social worlds and how they relate to the arena of teaching. 'A situational and social map could be seen as a to-ing and fro-ing between the empirical material level and interpretation level' (den Outer *et al.*, 2012: 15). In the diagram below, Luke is shown as belonging to several social worlds: he is a member of an Indigenous community, a teacher, an Indigenous teacher, and a husband. According to Clarke, 'there are multiple social worlds, and some overlap, demonstrating visually that some people and collectivities are participating in more than one. Similarly, certain social worlds are shown as participating in more than one arena' (Clarke, 2005: 111).

Figure 6.7: Social worlds/arenas map

Over the three years of the study, the social worlds in which Luke participated overlapped. Some were in tension with each other, some were foregrounded at particular times and others receded into the background. For example, for the first two years of Luke's career, his participation in the teaching arena as an Indigenous teacher was an important social world. His positioning by colleagues and school administrators first and foremost, as an 'Indigenous teacher', was a position he willingly took up. It may have provided him with significant levels of professional and personal fulfilment, appreciation from his colleagues as well as recognition and kudos from the Indigenous communities where the schools were located. However, the responsibilities he took on were far in excess of what might normally be expected of a novice teacher. There was a risk that such pressures could have led to burnout. His shift to Rosedale can be seen, in part, as a strategy of self-preservation – it may have enabled him to continue working as a teacher rather than risk burnout. There were few, if any, behaviour management problems at Rosedale and his work there was less demanding and less stressful than it had been at Boundary High or Crossthwaite High schools.

At about the same time, Luke's responsibilities as a husband become more significant and this social world began to come to the fore in the teaching arena. Tracey, who is unlikely to have had the same personal investment in Indigenous education, recognized the pressure her husband was under and encouraged him to move to Rosedale. Luke needed to consider his wife's values, aspirations and goals, as well as his own, and he may have realized that reducing the stress he was under was important for his relationship with Tracey. Luke's move to Rosedale enabled him to participate in the social world of being 'just a teacher' where his work was not connected to being Indigenous and he was treated just like he was one of the other teachers: a white teacher. Furthermore, being 'just a teacher' enabled him to take up a middle-class habitus, an identity he had been in the process of acquiring from the time he accessed higher education and the resultant cultural, economic and social capital (Bourdieu, 1987).

Prior to leaving home and attending university, Luke, like many of his family members and hometown peers, had access to limited economic, social and cultural capitals. His hometown, being similar to many rural Australian communities, was characterized by high levels of unemployment, low levels of education, low per capita income and relative geographical isolation. However, his completion of secondary school and then a university degree enabled him to access different capitals from those of his family and peers. His education enabled him to access cultural capital (valuable knowledge about how to 'succeed' in life), as well as monetary assets (economic capital), and powerful social capital (resources gained through membership of professional networks and related social relationships). In turn, economic capital provided him with choices and options about where he lived, his lifestyle and the personal relationships and networks he developed. By the time he took up a position at Rosedale, he was living in an expensive area of town, had married a successful professional white woman and had an urban lifestyle characterized by eating out and going on overseas holidays. It was these markers of social class that may have contributed to the teachers and students at Rosedale considering him to be a middle-class, and therefore 'white', teacher.

During the early part of his career and within the teaching arena, Luke was clearly located within the social world of an Indigenous person. However, his membership of this social world appeared to become less important after his move to Sydney. He was physically removed from his own Indigenous community, had married his non-Indigenous girlfriend, had moved to a predominantly white middle-class area of Sydney and by the end of year three, his Indigeneity was invisible to his colleagues, who saw him as just another white teacher. However, the fact that he says he feels guilty about not teaching Indigenous children, suggests that the social world of being an Indigenous person is enduring and continues to impact on the teaching arena in which he finds himself.

Conclusions

The answer to my question about why Luke moved to a school where there were no Indigenous students after having been deeply involved in Indigenous education for the first two years of his career is not straightforward. It seems that the shift was a result of the ongoing stress associated with the unrealistic workload connected to being 'the' Indigenous teacher in the school and having responsibility for all things Indigenous. I also speculate that it was shaped by his upward social class mobility and the increased choices about his lifestyle and career that were available to him. It is clear to me that the use of longitudinal research methodology enabled the changes to Luke's professional and personal life to be revealed over time. A singular one-hour interview would not have revealed the complex interplay of Luke's life events. However, it was situational analysis and its emphases on the human and the non-human contextual factors that contributed to my understanding of the tensions between different parts of Luke's self such as his Indigeneity and his social class, including his identity as a teacher, as a husband, as an Indigenous man, and within the settings of different schools and Indigenous and non-Indigenous communities. Situational analysis enabled me to become 'not only analyst and bricouler but also a cartographer of sorts' (Clarke, 2005: xxxvii).[3]

I suggest that situational analysis is useful for researchers working in culturally diverse contexts because it makes visible what might be beyond a researcher's normal field of vision and enables the identification of 'sites of silence' (Clarke, 2005). Those who research within culturally diverse sites where they are cultural outsiders are constantly challenged to find ways to understand lives and contexts shaped by cultures they do not know. By mapping key elements of a context, situational analysis makes these factors and the connections between them explicit. The construction of the Social Worlds/Arenas map has raised my awareness of how the worlds in which Luke participated intersected and overlapped in complex ways. Situational analysis also raises researchers' awareness of the need for reflective and reflexive research processes, 'prompting the researcher to reflect on the favouring of certain interpretations, existing multiplicity of interpretations of accounts, why certain worlds dominate over others, etc.' (den Outer *et al.*, 2012: 15). Research that seeks, in the interests of social justice, to question and disrupt existing asymmetrical relationships of power in culturally diverse social contexts needs to facilitate understandings of the range of human and non-human elements that can impact upon the situation under study.

References

Australian Bureau of Statistics (2011) '2011 Census Counts – Aboriginal and Torres Strait Islander Peoples'. Online. http://tinyurl.com/kxz7e6y (accessed May 2014).

Bourdieu, P. (1987) 'What makes a social class? On the theoretical and practical existence of groups'. *Berkeley Journal of Sociology*, 32, 1–17.

Clarke, A. (2005) *Situational Analysis: Grounded theory after the postmodern turn*. Thousand Oaks, CA: Sage.

Den Outer, B., Handley, K. and Price, M. (2012) 'Situational analysis and mapping for use in education research: A reflexive methodology?' *Studies in Higher Education*, 38 (10), 1–18.

Elliot, J. (2005) *Using Narrative in Social Research*. Thousand Oaks, CA: Sage.

Haggis, T. (2009) 'What have we been thinking of? A critical overview of 40 years of student learning research in higher education'. *Studies in Higher Education*, 34 (4), 377–90.

Hughes, P. and Willmot, E. (1982) 'A thousand Indigenous teachers by 1990'. In Sherwood, E. (ed.) *Aboriginal Education: Issues and innovations*. Perth, Australia: Creative Research, 45–9.

Khaw, L. (2012) 'Mapping the Process: An exemplar of using situational analysis in a grounded theory study'. *Journal of Family Theory and Review*, 4, 138–47.

Llewellyn, P. and Northway, R. (2007) 'The views and experiences of learning disability nurses concerning their advocacy education'. *Nurse Education Today*, 27, 955–63.

Mills, J., Francis, F. and Bonner, B. (2008) 'Getting to know a stranger – rural nurses' experiences of mentoring: A grounded theory'. *International Journal of Nursing Studies*, 45, 599–607.

Nelson, J. and Gould, J. (2005) 'Hidden in the mirror: A reflective conversation about research with marginalized communities'. *Reflective Practice*, 6 (3), 327–39.

Reid, J., Santoro, N., Crawford, L. and Simpson, L. (2009) 'Talking teacher education: Factors impacting on teacher education for Indigenous people'. *Australian Journal of Indigenous Education*, 38, 42–54.

Reissman, C.K. (2008) *Narrative Methods for the Human Sciences*. Thousand Oaks, CA: Sage.

Santoro, N., Reid, J., Crawford, L. and Simpson, L. (2011) 'Teaching Indigenous children: Listening to and learning from Indigenous teachers'. *Australian Journal of Teacher Education*, 36 (10), 65–76.

Santoro, N. (2010) '"If it weren't for my mum …": The influence of Australian Indigenous mothers on their children's aspirations to teach'. *Gender and Education*, 22 (4) 419–29.

— (2013) '"I really want to make a difference for these kids but it's just too hard": One Aboriginal teacher's experiences of moving away, moving on and moving up'. *International Journal of Qualitative Studies in Education*, 26 (8), 953–66.

Endnotes

[1] Indigenous Australians are First Nations people from mainland Australia and the Torres Straits, an island territory north of Australia. They have a history predating European settlement in Australia by more than 40,000 years. At the last census, Indigenous people comprised 2.5 per cent of the Australian population (Australian Bureau of Statistics, 2011).

[2] Australian Indigenous people usually identify themselves as belonging to a particular tribal area or nation. I have foregrounded this information when referring to Luke for the first time. Wiradjuri nation extends over much of the Australian state of New South Wales and has one of the largest populations of Indigenous people in Australia. Wiradjuri people, like all Indigenous peoples, have a distinct language and culture.

[3] This chapter explicates the methods of analysis used in the paper published in *International Journal of Qualitative Studies in Education*. Further details of the findings, discussion and implications can be found in Santoro, 2013.

Chapter 7
Participatory action research in a high school drama club: A catalyst for change among English language learners in Canada
Antoinette Gagné and Stephanie Soto Gordon

Introduction
Through their involvement in a high school drama club, immigrant English language learners (ELLs) and Canadian-born fluent English speakers (CFESs) were given the opportunity to improve their quality of life by creating a series of DVDs related to their interaction experiences. These students became action researchers using critical pedagogy as a framework. The research was 'guided by passion and principle, to help students develop consciousness of freedom, recognize authoritarian tendencies, and connect knowledge to power and the ability to take constructive action' (Giroux, 2010: 1).

The three-phase action research project had four clear aims:

- to provide a personal growth opportunity for a group of teenaged ELLs and CFESs while empowering them as agents of change
- to explore the experiences of teenage immigrants in high school
- to uncover the nature of the relationships between them and their Canadian-born peers in a secondary school and in the community beyond
- and to examine the impact of this collaborative project on the participants.

Our research was action oriented at first and driven by our concerns related to the often difficult experiences of ELLs in secondary schools. However, the diverse student participants gradually took the reins and determined the direction of the research, aiming to improve their quality of life at school. As all three phases of the project were embedded in the overall activities of the school, the administration required that a teacher sponsor the action research. As we progressed through the phases, we provided less and less scaffolding as the students increasingly assumed leadership in determining the goals of the research. Accordingly, the project could be characterized as participatory action research. The student-researchers initially lacked confidence in themselves, but through the project they became strong advocates for themselves and other students, whether they were born in Canada or new to the country.

Our research included the development of three DVDs (Gagné, 2006, 2007, 2010) and a resource book (Gagné, 2008) in the *Growing New Roots* series, which addresses issues of diversity as they pertain to immigrant English language learners and their families. Each of the DVDs was produced collaboratively with a number of field partners. The focus of the series is very practical and its intent is to allow immigrant families, teen ELLs and their CFES peers, and their teachers, to share their experiences and related insights on the integration process.

Funding came from small-scale grants encouraging partnerships between the university and the community. Each grant allocated funds for research and also for the development of DVDs. Our main partner in the project was the Toronto District School Board, which is the largest in Canada and also has the most diverse student population.

Research methodology

More than 30 ELLs aged 14 to 18, from a wide range of language proficiency levels and countries of origin, as well as a dozen CFES students, were involved in different phases of the project in one high school. In the first two years, mainly Grade 10 ELLs were involved. About 20 ELLs, who had been in Canada for six to 12 months, participated in the ESL Drama class in Phase 1 and worked towards the production of the first DVD, entitled *Growing New Roots: The voices of immigrant teens in Canada* (Gagné, 2006). This first DVD focuses on their expectations of immigration, their challenges in a new high school, their strategies for coping, and their suggestions for teachers.

During Phase 2, in the ESL Drama Club, ELLs who had heard about the project joined several of the students from Phase 1. The students filmed in the second DVD, entitled *Growing New Roots: Reflections of immigrant teenagers in Canada* (Gagné, 2007), had been in Canada for about 18 to 24 months. In the second DVD, the ELLs speak about relationships with family and friends, and aspects of school life including alienation and racism, as well as the importance of active involvement at school.

The participants in the third phase of the project were ELLs and CFESs of English in Grades 10 to 12, and they produced a DVD entitled *Growing New Roots: Coming together – new immigrant and Canadian teenagers* (Gagné, 2010). The ELLs were members of the ESL Drama Club who had shown an interest in talking about the challenges of interacting with CFESs, and the CFES students had been recommended by teachers who knew them to be caring. This highlights the experience of coming together and learning to form a community. The participants describe the barriers they encountered to interacting with the other group and suggest solutions to overcome such obstacles for students, parents and educators.

Guided by critical pedagogy, and with the permission of the parents and the support of the principal, the authors – Antoinette Gagné from the University of Toronto and Stephanie Soto Gordon, the ESL drama teacher and drama club sponsor – worked for five years with the students to prepare short skits and narratives focusing on the challenges they had faced in and out of school and how they had worked through them to achieve a positive outcome. Guided by some questions, students reflected on their personal immigration and integration experiences, and shared their experiences with the other participants in the club or class. Towards the end of each year, the students were asked to reflect on the impact of working together to prepare the content of the DVD. The research findings were then integrated into various resources to facilitate the use of the DVD series across a range of settings, including teacher education programmes, community centres and secondary school classrooms.

Action research and participatory action research

The research methodology initially adopted was action research; however, it evolved into participatory action research. Action research may be defined as research conducted by teachers for teachers: 'it can inform teachers about their practice and empower them to take leadership roles in their contexts ... the information is gathered with the goals of gaining insight, developing reflective practice, effecting positive changes in the environment and on educational practices in general, and improving student outcomes' (Mills, 2003: 4). Reason (1994) expands this definition to include empowering the participants through the process of constructing and using their own knowledge and this then is participatory action research. O'Leary (2004) asserts that participatory action research can allow the oppressed to produce knowledge and determine the nature of change interventions to emancipate themselves. Thus a key difference between the two is that in action research, the researcher leads, whereas in participatory action research, the researcher assumes the role of facilitator, the participants drive the research and are empowered through the process as they gain knowledge and promote change.

Although there are many definitions of action research, our experience with a diverse group of student-researchers in one secondary school in Toronto is best defined by Reason and Bradbury as:

> a participatory, democratic process concerned with developing practical knowing in the pursuit of worthwhile human purposes, grounded in a participatory worldview that is currently emerging at this historical moment. It seeks to bring together action and reflection, theory and practice, in participation with others, in the pursuit of practical solutions to issues of pressing concern to people, and more generally the flourishing of individual persons and their communities.
>
> (Reason and Bradbury, 2001: 1)

Phase 1: Growing New Roots: The voices of immigrant teens in Canada

The motivation for creating the first DVD emerged from Stephanie Soto Gordon's experiences in the classroom with her ELLs. Her students would talk to her informally about their expectations of Canada, and how their new reality did not always reflect those expectations. They would discuss the challenges they faced and their strategies for coping with them. Such conversations inspired Stephanie to invite immigrant students to share their stories, in the hope that educators would use their new awareness of the ELLs' experiences to adapt their teaching practice and create a culture of empathy that could ultimately improve students' achievement. It was important to make sure that even the voices of ELLs with limited proficiency in English could be heard, as they had much of value to contribute to the project.

Phase 2: Growing New Roots: Reflections of immigrant teenagers in Canada

Antoinette and Stephanie recognized that the ELLs in the first DVD had been truly empowered by its creation and so were committed to continue collaborating on the creation of a second DVD. The ELLs had frequently told their teachers how their active participation in the creation of a video available on a university website had made them realize that they had information and expertise that teachers who work with immigrant teens needed. They could inform educators about the challenges of sponsored immigration faced by teenagers and suggest effective strategies to support them. The participants were proud to know that their DVD had been viewed by educators across the Toronto area as well as by many online at the ESL Infusion website. They reported feeling how they were transformed from feeling vulnerable in the school because of their newcomer status, to feeling strong because of their ability to help other immigrant students by creating a climate of change to support the implementation of inclusive education practices in their school and beyond. The ELLs describe these feelings of transformation and empowerment at the end of the second DVD. One ELL who had been in Canada for less than two years when they took part in the project said: 'Before this activity, I was afraid to talk to people, I didn't trust myself, and I didn't like to go out with anybody', and another that 'After this activity, I will be very happy because I will make other people understand us and the way we feel. And the most important thing is that now I believe in myself.'

As the second project progressed, the ELLs who had been involved in the first phase took on leadership roles as directors of the second DVD. Now veterans, they helped to raise awareness about the importance of participation and supported the newer ELL participants as they prepared and presented their ideas. Stephanie's role shifted to that of facilitator, in which she followed the lead of the ELLs as they determined the topics to explore and ensured that each ELL felt themselves valued as a contributor to the cause of educating the educators. There had clearly been a power shift from educators to ELLs because of the project, which had transitioned from action research to participatory action research.

Phase 3: Growing New Roots: Coming together – new immigrant and Canadian teenagers

During the second phase of the project, the findings of a more formal study involving ELLs in multilevel secondary school ESL classrooms became the driving force behind the third DVD (Soto Gordon, 2010). Lave and Wenger's (1991) community of practice framework and Dörnyei and Ottó's (1998) conceptual framework for motivation to learn an additional language were used as analytical lenses. Results indicated that the various characteristics of multilevel classrooms could affect student participation and motivation in either a positive or negative manner. The participants in this study identified themselves as central in determining the degree to which they participated in class and were motivated to learn English. In addition, the ELL participants repeatedly described challenging issues around their interaction with CFES students in mainstream classrooms. In fact, during several interviews, one participant called for educators to raise awareness about the separation of immigrant students from CFES because 'the school was too divided' (Soto Gordon, 2010). These comments became a call to action that led to the creation of a third DVD where students once again determined the content.

At the beginning of the third phase, many immigrant students at the high school were already aware of the ELL DVD project and were interested in getting involved in raising awareness about their lives as teenage newcomers. The third DVD project empowered the participants in two ways. First, it afforded them the opportunity to provide expert information on the challenges faced by ELLs and CFESs when interacting, as well as strategies for improving the quality of education in highly diverse settings. Second, it created a context where their feelings of vulnerability were decreased. Through their participation in the third phase of this project, the ways that ELLs and CFES participants related to each other were transformed.

Deconstructing the research process: nested pedagogical orientations model

Cummins's (2009) model of nested pedagogical orientations helps to explain the transition from action research to participatory action research from Phase 1 to Phase 3 of this project. In this model, Cummins positions transmission-oriented pedagogy in an inner circle with the narrowest focus, because its goal is to transmit information and skills specified in the curriculum directly to students. Social constructivist pedagogy is placed in the middle pedagogical space, as it seeks to include the development of higher-order thinking among learners, based on the co-construction of knowledge by teachers. It thus moves beyond the mere transmission of the prescribed curriculum. Cummins points out that transformative approaches to pedagogy go beyond the other pedagogies by enabling students to learn how knowledge, social realities and power relations are interconnected.

In Phase 1 of the project, Stephanie's action research orientation complemented her social constructivist pedagogy as an ESL teacher and Drama Club sponsor. However, the outcomes of Phase 1 of the project proved transformative not only for the students but also for their teacher and club sponsor. She embraced a more participatory form of action research in the remaining two phases of the project. As she observed the positive effects of participation on her students and their willingness to take on active leadership roles, she adopted an ever more transformative pedagogical orientation while becoming more of a research facilitator.

Participatory action research

Figure 7.1: Nested pedagogical orientations (diagram adapted with the permission of Jim Cummins)

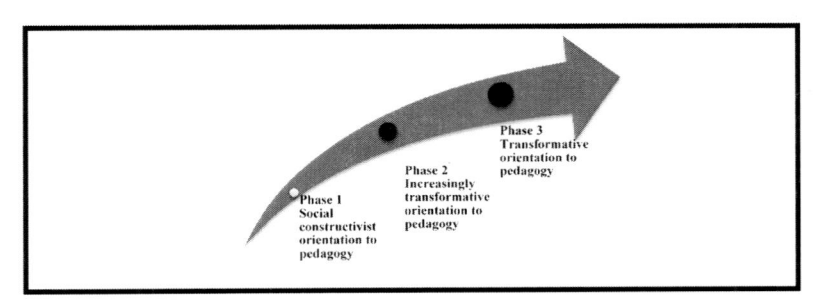

Figure 7.2: Evolution of Stephanie's orientation to pedagogy

Opportunities and challenges

In the next section we consider aspects of the action research process experienced over phases of the project, and explore the opportunities and challenges presented. Recommendations follow, based on our experiences when working with these ethnically and linguistically diverse high school students.

Consent and retention

In Phases 1 and 2 of the project, only letters of consent and media releases were required to begin the action research. The time from project inception to completion did not take many months, and encouraged a high level of student retention. In order to move into Phase 3, however, an ethical review was required at both the level of the university and the school district. As the ethics review application forms were submitted sequentially, it took several months to obtain approval to conduct research, so the retention rate of participants for Phase 3 was significantly lower because some of the students who had expressed interest in participating got involved in other activities while others fell away for reasons such as moving school. We learned how important it is to explain the timeline at the beginning of the project so that immigrant students are not too disappointed if they cannot participate because of the length of time required.

The first DVD production was integrated into the Drama curriculum, so rehearsals were scheduled in class time. The retention rate for this phase was high because no other activities competed with the project-based workshops or rehearsals. It is important to be aware of the various constraints immigrant students have on their time. Many are required to assist parents as translators or babysitters, and they may have part-time jobs to help support their families as they settle in their new homeland. So integrating action research into particular courses makes it easier for the students to take part.

As the second and third phases of the project were not embedded in a course and a certain amount of preparation for workshops and rehearsals was required, a few of the student-researchers could not complete this preparatory work or attend some of the meetings or rehearsals, while others decided that the project was too demanding and dropped out. The research facilitator must be mindful of the time required for the student-researchers to complete preparation work and attend workshops or rehearsals and ensure that the minority ethnic participants are not jeopardizing their academic achievement or losing out on other extra-curricular activities such as sports teams, clubs or a part-time job – all of which are important to students and especially to immigrant students.

We concluded that shorter projects that require involvement for six months or less are more viable for newcomers, because many of them move from one school to another in the process of settlement. With a short timeline, it is more likely that immigrant students who express interest in the project will be able to see it through.

Recruitment of participants and community building

Although the student researchers did not reflect the full range of diversity among the students at the school, they were very diverse in their countries of origin, language proficiency, age, religion and socio-economic status.

Most were ELLs in an ESL Drama class and members of a Drama Club, so were interested in acting. In these sheltered classes and clubs, newcomers already felt a sense of security and kinship with their peers and could be comfortable sharing personal challenges about their immigration, so they were ideal participants in the project.

Their teachers selected the CFES participants whom they perceived to be sensitive to the needs of ELLs. The recruitment of CFES students thus recruited showed genuine interest in understanding the experiences of immigrants, so readily committed to the project and were open about the challenges they encountered when interacting with the newcomers. The two groups quickly built rapport and evoked an atmosphere of trust. They all felt safe in exposing their vulnerability about interacting with each other and building community.

The student-researchers' commitment

The student-researchers brought energy and passion to the project as they became motivated to share their stories and work together to create a more inclusive learning environment at the school. Their motivation and interest in the project grew when they learned about the impact the first DVD had had beyond their own school. They were eager to begin work on Phase 2 now that they realized the power of their immigration and integration experiences and of their suggestions for improvement when they presented them compellingly in video. Their confidence grew and they perceived themselves as ambassadors for other minority students and agents of change. They also saw that their involvement in the project enhanced their resumés and added this experience to their applications to college or university.

Sensitive topics

It was important that all the adults involved in the project across phases were sensitive to the fact that the topics explored were emotionally charged for the diverse group of student-researchers, and we called on the same adults to be involved in the research if they could. For example, when the videographer who had worked with the participants in Phase 1 was available for Phase 2, both the students and the teacher were more relaxed about the filming. The need to build trust between the adults involved and among immigrant and CFES student-researchers is the key to the success of a project that addresses sensitive issues and the challenges presented by acquiring proficiency in English. Some participants became emotional during the workshops and rehearsals, so the adults working with them had to be vigilant and know about the services available to support them in the school so they could provide help when needed.

As the participants were sometimes concerned about how others might react to their narratives or comments, it was important to make it clear from the start that they could be about any information, ideas, or experiences they chose to share. Protecting the emotional well-being of the student-researchers was the paramount concern, so sensitivity training was integrated into the initial workshops of each phase.

Editing the videos

To ensure that the immigrant student-researchers felt their feedback and contributions were valued, the film crew needed to consult with them and listen to their suggestions at all stages of the process. That the students were from the same technological generation as the film crew meant they felt comfortable giving feedback to the crew. Such collaboration is a crucial feature of participatory action research.

Although it is good practice to elicit feedback from participants at every stage of a project, it was sometimes difficult to do so with the final production of each video because of the time lapse between filming and editing. As the participants knew many technological applications that allow instant viewing of video footage, it was necessary to explain the process of editing and the time required to create a high-quality video product. With these vulnerable students it was important that the video editors worked closely with one of the facilitators to ensure that the messages the participants wanted to communicate came across clearly in the final production.

With the student-researchers in charge of determining the content of the videos, we were concerned about the possibility of stereotypes emerging, but saw it as unlikely when the participants were from such diverse backgrounds. Although it was tempting to edit the footage captured to eliminate some linguistic errors or overgeneralizations, we chose rather to respect the student-researchers' work.

Although limited English proficiency was a challenge for some participants, they opted to use English even when given the opportunity to speak in their mother tongue and have a peer translate. Several of the participants reported that speaking in English helped with their new identity as immigrants to Canada. Both the CFESs and the ELLs felt safe during the filming because they knew that any segment could be filmed more than once to remove any embarrassing mistakes. The filming and editing process allowed the participants from minority backgrounds to feel comfortable sharing their opinions even if they made a mistake, because they knew it could be changed.

During each phase of the project, controversial issues were raised that sometimes caused tensions about how to honour the participants' voices. So we had to allow enough time during editing to get feedback from the student researchers while upholding university and board of education policies related to such issues as privacy, student safety and equity. We had to explain these policies to the student-researchers so they understood why some comments might need to be edited.

Power differential
In her multiple roles as teacher, club advisor and researcher, Stephanie got to know the student-researchers quite well. She tried to understand their complex lives and to ensure that their voices were heard at every stage. So in the first phase, for instance, ELLs were collaborative partners in determining the guiding research questions and eventual themes explored in the videos.

Most of the student-researchers knew her before the project began, and she was careful not to misuse her position of trust in workshops where sensitive topics were often discussed. As she was known to be an advocate for students, most felt comfortable disclosing their feelings in her presence and their bond with her grew and they called her 'Mama Soto'. Stephanie shared her own struggles and experiences when she had lived abroad and repeatedly told the student-researchers how interested she was in their stories and how important it was that these were shared, along with their suggestions for creating a more inclusive school environment.

Dissemination of findings
As an ESL teacher and curriculum leader, Stephanie could easily keep the school community informed about the project and to increase educators' awareness about the ELLs' and CFESs' experiences in the hope that classroom teachers would improve the learning conditions for other newcomers.

Antoinette's role as collaborator, university-based researcher and teacher educator gave her access to sources of funding for these costly projects. Having been involved in the design and implementation of several research projects with immigrant participants that culminated in video productions, Antoinette brought a practical perspective to the project and saw to it that the videos and related resources could easily be integrated with courses or workshops for teachers working in other diverse schools. The additional resources available online include transcripts of the videos and a resource guide with activities for teacher educators and teachers to assist their understanding of the issues faced by immigrant students and indicate ways to create a more inclusive classroom and school environment.

One of the key roles Antoinette played was in raising the profile of the three-phase action research project through various dissemination activities such as workshops for teachers, conference presentations, and the inclusion of the videos and related resources online at the ESL Infusion website.

Outcomes

The benefits of participation for student-researchers from immigrant backgrounds

The student-researchers, whether ELL or CFES, benefitted from their involvement in the project in several ways:

- they improved their English and intercultural communication skills;
- they became more confident and learned the power of their words;
- they developed friendships with students from other backgrounds with whom they would probably not have otherwise mixed at school;
- they learned the value of becoming involved in school activity beyond the classroom.

As a teacher and department head, as well as the Drama Club advisor at the school throughout the project, Stephanie observed the student participants' academic and social growth. Although they have graduated, many stay in touch with her, which has allowed her to share the joy of knowing the impact of their participation on their future lives.

Before they took part in the project, few of the immigrant student-researchers were aware of the value placed on co-curricular involvement in Canadian society. For many of them, succeeding at school meant getting good grades and completing the academic requirements while working to help their families financially.

Through participatory action research, the student-researchers were able to see the project move from idea to product. They gained a sense of what is possible and of how they could interact with each other and begin to contribute to Canadian society. ELLs and CFESs described how participating in the latest project affected their identity. One ELL captures her empowering experience:

> Before, I was afraid of starting a conversation with other students other than ESL students, but now, I am not afraid to express myself. It was helpful to finally hear and see different perspectives of the native speakers and get to know them – something that I couldn't do before due to various reasons: shyness, fear of not

being understood, or make a mistake, or not having a good level of English to speak fluently.

Another said:

> I felt and thought differently on native students, because when you get to know a person beyond 'hi' and 'bye', suddenly all the anti, judgemental thoughts are going away.

A third newcomer said:

> We had different activities with the native speakers that encouraged me to learn about the Canadian culture. This process gave me more confidence to get involved and meet new and other people. It showed me that it is possible to get out from the 'ESL bubble' ... This experience helped me to understand that native speakers are willing to be friends with newcomers. Before, I was afraid of starting a conversation with other students other than ESL students, but now, I am not afraid to express myself.

CFES students also described positive experiences: 'It was a good experience to have to meet new people and talk to them about anything. It taught me that we are all very similar as well as unique.' Another said:

> I've really earned an understanding as to why English language learners appear to be defensive when I first meet them. I have many English language learners that I am good friends with. At the beginning though, I thought most of them were just not talkative and ignorant in nature. I never knew that for some, it is a very big difference coming to a new country.

Research facilitators

We facilitators have gained experience in leading from the front and from behind. After the project was initiated, the student-researchers took the lead, while we moved back to be a support. The participatory action research paradigm allowed us to honour the students' opinions and try to diminish the power imbalance between educators and students.

We learned that we needed to take a greater leadership role in the initial stages and allow time for the student-researchers to become confident about their language proficiency and the value of their stories. However, once student-researchers began to take the lead, the facilitators had to relinquish control and allow the students' voices to become the driving force.

During the three years we learned that student researchers might, for a range of reasons, lose focus and struggle to complete the project, and that we had to be prepared to step back into a more active leadership role and provide direction from time to time until they were able to take back the reigns and complete their project.

Our work with adolescent students from diverse backgrounds has reinforced our belief that all students, including immigrant students, can be transformed by their involvement in participatory action research. When their voices are heard by their teachers and other adults and this effects change in their learning environment, their confidence grows and they find that their actions have indeed been worthwhile.

References

Cummins, J. (2009) 'Pedagogies of choice: Challenging coercive relations of power in classrooms and communities'. *International Journal of Bilingual Education and Bilingualism*, 12, 261–72.

Dörnyei, Z. and Ottó, I. (1998) 'Motivation in action: A process model of L2 motivation'. *Working Papers in Applied Linguistics*, 4, 43–69.

Gagné, A. (ed.) (2007) *Growing New Roots: The voices of immigrant families and the teachers of their children. Resource book for educators and immigrant families.* Toronto: Ontario Institute for Studies in Education, University of Toronto.

— (producer) (2006) *Growing New Roots: The voices of immigrant teens.* DVD (10 minutes). Toronto: Ontario Institute for Studies in Education, University of Toronto.

— (producer) (2007) *Growing New Roots: Reflections of immigrant teenagers in Canada.* DVD. Toronto: Ontario Institute for Studies in Education, University of Toronto.

— (ed.) (2008) *Growing New Roots: The voices and reflections of immigrant teens – resource book for educators, English language learners and immigrant teens.* Toronto: Ontario Institute for Studies in Education, University of Toronto.

— (producer) (2010) *Growing New Roots: Coming together – new immigrant and Canadian teenagers.* DVD. Ontario Institute for Studies in Education, University of Toronto.

Giroux, H. (2010) 'Lessons from Paulo Freire'. *The Chronicle of Higher Education.* 15 November, 2010. Online. http://chronicle.com/article/Lessons-From-Paulo-Freire/124910/ (requires subscription).

Lave, J. and Wenger, E. (1991) *Situated Learning: Legitimate peripheral participation.* New York: Cambridge University Press.

Mills, G.E. (2003) *Action Research: A guide for the teacher researcher.* Upper Saddle River, NJ: Merrill Prentice Hall.

O'Leary, Z. (2004) *The Essential Guide to Doing Research.* London: Sage.

Reason, P. and Bradbury, H. (2001) *Handbook of Action Research: Participative inquiry and practice.* London: Sage.

Reason, P. (1994) 'Three approaches to participative inquiry'. In Denzin, N.K. and Lincoln, Y.S. (eds) *Handbook of Qualitative Research*. Thousand Oaks, CA: Sage, 324–39.

Soto Gordon, S. (2010) 'A case study on multi-level language ability groupings in an ESL secondary school classroom: Are we making the right choices?' Doctoral diss., University of Toronto.

Chapter 8
Children's agency in research: Does photography empower participants?
Giovanna Fassetta

Introduction

This chapter explores the use of photography by children to gather data in research. It considers the technique from a reflexive standpoint (Pink, 2003) to evaluate the extent to which it can effectively empower children. More specifically, it discusses the use of cameras by children who took part in a research project on migration. Throughout the chapter, I refer to the technique as 'child-led' or 'participant-led' photography (Gallagher, 2008; Fassetta, 2010).

The choice of child-led photography for data collection is usually grounded in a rationale aimed at involving children in the process as competent actors, in order for research to be *with* children rather than *on* children (James, 2007). As technical equipment has become more widely available, photography has grown increasingly popular in research with participants of all ages (Pink, 2003; Banks, 2007). Predominantly employed in the context of qualitative research, this technique is often chosen in studies that involve young participants, as it is expected to reveal the world as 'seen through the eyes of children' (Banks, 2007: 5). This is particularly desirable given that young people's interests and points of view are often ignored, or have a secondary role within research.

The unequal power relations that characterize adult–child interactions can be replicated in the researcher–participant encounter, as young people are used to complying with adults' requests. This can be especially noticeable when research is conducted in an institution such as a school, where young people are expected to behave according to rules determined and enforced by adults (Morgan *et al.*, 2002). Several authors (Punch, 2002; Langevang, 2007; Clark, 2010; Oh, 2012) propose that the adoption of participatory techniques can help to redress the power imbalance and give children an active role in the research process. Through photography children can be engaged directly in the data collection and thus involved as co-researchers and knowledge-makers.

The chapter outlines the aims of the study discussed and highlights issues of agency and power inequalities that commonly arise in research with young participants. It discusses the difficulties faced when analysing visual data and the dynamics and processes that influence children's choices of subject when using a camera in a research context. The positive aspects of the technique are considered and suggestions made regarding ways to maximize its potential.

My decision to concentrate primarily on the challenges of photography for data collection does not reflect a value assessment of the technique. I aim instead to redress a tendency to focus primarily on the benefits, and to ensure that both advantages and potential issues are openly acknowledged and discussed, to allow photography to be chosen in full awareness of its value as a tool for research.

Children, agency and power imbalance

The research project involved 41 participants (30 girls and 11 boys) between the ages of 10 and 15 who had had direct or indirect experience of migration. The study explored how children imagine a country of which they have no first-hand experience, but to which they have links through significant others; it also investigated the role this (imagined) country plays in young people's expectations for the future. The study comprised three groups of children: a group left in Ghana by parents who had migrated to Italy and who expected to move there soon on family reunion visas; a group of young people born in Italy of Ghanaian parents; and a group of children who had recently (within a four-year timeframe) moved to join their families in Italy, and who, consequently, were able to assess the expectations and imaginings held prior to migration in the light of the encounter with the 'real' country. The main aim of the research was to add the narratives of young people to the debate on migration, a perspective that is too often absent from the conversation, even though large numbers of migrants are children (Suárez-Orozco and Suárez-Orozco, 2001).

While children are deeply affected by adult decisions that can be life changing, such as that of relocating to a new country, they seldom have the means to resist or challenge these choices. The widespread assumption that children are human 'becomings' whose lives are to be seen primarily as a time of apprenticeship for adulthood has however been challenged over the past two decades (Holloway and Valentine, 2000; Tisdall and Punch,

2012). Childhood is now recognized as a socially constructed category that is geographically and historically bound but which is, nevertheless, a permanent feature of society (James and James, 2004). This has led to growing concern with how children actively engage in everyday life, and an interest in understanding young people's perceptions by directly involving them in the research process.

Including young people as active participants in research can help to redress their marginalization and subordination by allowing them to contribute to knowledge-making. However, the necessity of ensuring that children are safe and cared for at all times means that their well-being is the responsibility of adults. While essential to children's welfare, this also has implications for research, as young participants can only be included after negotiation with adult gatekeepers (e.g. parents/carers and/or teachers, headteachers, social workers) who have the ultimate say over whether they take part in a research study (Catts *et al.*, 2007). This poses questions about the basis of children's participation, and raises important ethical issues, such as how we can be sure that the children's choice to take part in research reflects their wishes and not those of their parents, carers or guardians. Would most children feel that they are able to refuse to cooperate with the request of an adult simply by being reassured that they are free to do so? To what extent are children captive participants, and can this ever be otherwise? These are issues that all research, be it with children or adults, needs to confront, at least to some extent. Young people's involvement amplifies these ethical dilemmas as their participation is always subordinate to adults' written consent, a circumstance that lays bare the fact that choosing whether or not to take part in research may not be a real option for many young people (Sime, 2008; Fassetta, 2010).

It is also important to note that 'childhood' is not a homogeneous category but one in which other social categories (e.g. gender, class, ethnicity, religious affiliation) intersect, hence making 'children' a composite and diverse group (Holloway and Valentine, 2000). Since children are gendered, classed and racialized beings, their agency, experiences, expectations and concerns are subject to the specific limitations of their group memberships and can also be affected by the way in which these limitations combine (Crenshaw, 1991; Nash, 2008; Fassetta, 2013).

As Langevang notes, 'when the research participants are young Africans and the researcher an adult European, unequal power relations between the researcher and the researched are intensified and need to be reflected upon during the research process' (2007: 269). While such power imbalance cannot be entirely avoided, it is important that researchers acknowledge the issues this poses, rather than avoiding them or pretending that a particular methodology will suffice to restore equilibrium (Kothari, 2001; Gallacher and Gallagher, 2008). Nevertheless, some techniques can, if used thoughtfully and in full awareness of their weaknesses, help to redress the unequal control over the research process. Child-led photography is one of the techniques that can allow participants more control, but its limitations and challenges must be recognized.

The promises of child-led photography

The choice to use child-led photography as one of the data collection techniques to explore children's expectations and experiences of migration was made primarily in an effort to engage the children as active co-researchers and thus to redress, as far as possible, the imbalance of power that exists between adult-researcher and child-participants (Young and Barrett, 2001; Punch, 2002; Barker and Weller, 2003; Ortega-Alcázar and Dyck, 2012). I also judged that this activity would be more fun and less like schoolwork (Barker and Weller, 2003; Clark-Ibáñez, 2007; Enright and O'Sullivan, 2012), thus avoiding a teacher–pupil interaction. Moreover, I believed that, since the photographs would be taken without my physical presence, the children would have more control over the data collection and feel less pressure to perform (Young and Barrett, 2001). I intended to use the photographs to shape and sustain the subsequent individual interviews by guiding the exchange between adult and children, providing something to talk about, and helping with possible language difficulties (Barker and Weller, 2003; Dodman, 2003; Oh, 2012).

While several of these expectations were sustained by the practice, there were also unanticipated challenges that made me review the technique critically. In the next section I examine the dilemmas that using participant-led photography can pose researchers, while keeping sight of the positive aspects. Although the issues and questions I highlight are not restricted to research with young participants, the imbalance of power means that concerns are magnified by the fact that young people may feel pressured into complying with adult requests. When the participants are young African immigrants, their youth can combine with their minority status to make them even more unlikely to challenge the requests of a white Italian adult (Santoro and Smyth, 2010). Finally, the western researcher's attempt to understand other cultures can come up against preconceptions and stereotyping of the 'Other' grounded in Western hegemonic discourses (Spivak, 1988; Said, 1978), an eventuality that researchers cannot afford to discount.

I collected data in Italy and Ghana (between October 2008 and May 2009) using a variety of techniques selected and combined for their potential to maximize children's active participation. Following the initial meeting with the young people during focus group interviews, each participant was given a disposable camera with which to take pictures of geographical or social similarities or differences between Ghana and Italy. The children were then met once more, individually, to talk through the photographs taken and to re-visit some of the issues that had been discussed during the focus groups.

Precautions were taken to ensure that the children were as involved as possible in the data collection as informed and consenting individuals and, at the same time, that they would be safe while taking the photographs (Langevang, 2007). The participants were offered the cameras and reassured that they were free *not* to take them, but all took up the offer. They were shown how to use the cameras and told to make sure they asked for consent before taking close-ups of people (ibid.). After a week, the cameras were collected, the films developed, and two sets of photographs were printed, one for the children and one for the researcher. At the individual interviews, the children were given time to look through my set of photographs in order to remove any image they were not happy to talk about or for me to have (Clark-Ibáñez, 2007).

What exactly are we seeing?

My expectation was that allowing the young participants to take the pictures without my presence would mean that they could select what they thought most closely portrayed their expectations and experiences. Accordingly, I asked the children in Ghana and the children born in Italy of Ghanaian parents to photograph anything (places, objects, people, activities, etc.) in their daily lives that they thought would be similar or different in the other country (i.e. Ghana for those in Italy, Italy for those in Ghana). As neither group had direct experience of the other country, I expected that the choice of subjects would give me an insight into the children's imaginings and expectations. The children who had recently moved between the two countries, on the other hand, were asked to take pictures of anything that they had found to be as they had expected, or different, surprising or unusual in any way. Since these participants had direct knowledge of both countries, I expected their images would portray their own appraisal of their imaginings, and reveal their experiences as young migrants.

Following the children's selection, I was left with a total of 584 photographs. I had anticipated being able to code the great number of pictures I had available on the basis of the children's comments and, to this

Using photography

end, I noted their remarks on the back of each photograph. The resulting themes and subthemes, I envisaged, would reveal which aspects of the two countries the children consider most relevant, together with the foci of their expectations, concerns and experiences.

However, while coding the photographs taken by the children in Italy, I saw a more complex picture emerge. The following were the main, 'grand' themes that emerged from the data collected in Italy:

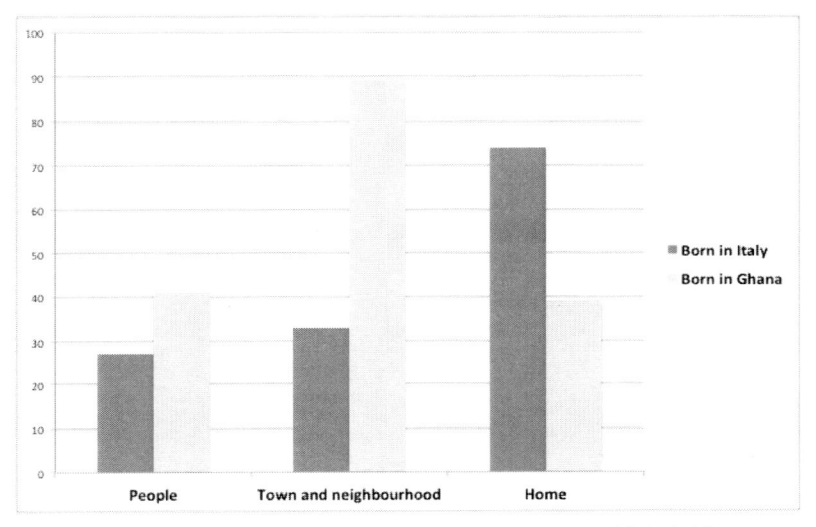

Figure 8.1: Subjects of children's photographs categorized by child's birthplace

There were clearly quite substantial variations in the subjects for the children born in Italy and the children who had moved from Ghana to Italy. The first group appeared to have focused principally on the home (furniture and objects), while the second group had concentrated more on the immediate surroundings of the neighbourhood and, to a lesser extent, on aspects of the town. This seems to indicate different foci of interest for the two groups, with the migrant children showing greater interest in the 'exterior' of places, and the children born in Italy finding more similarities and differences within the confines of the home. What both groups shared, however, was the relative lack of photographs that portrayed people. The few that did depict people showed either members of the immediate family, some of them posing to model a traditional Ghanaian dress or hair-do, or friends in their Sunday outfits. A very small number of participants had taken pictures of their Italian classmates and none of them had taken pictures of white Italian people (whether children or adults) outside the school. The vast majority of the photographs were taken in or around the house.

The images of the immediate neighbourhood were often shot from the home's balcony or window, as the picture in Figure 8.2 by a 12-year-old participant exemplifies.

> This is XX, my friend. He was waiting for me and so I took his picture from our balcony. You can see our garage over there.
> Marty, male, age 12, Italy

Figure 8.2: From the balcony

This can indicate that the home and the neighbourhood are places that resonate deeply with the children, and that people are somewhat less significant subjects (Sharples *et al.*, 2003). However, it is also possible that the choice of these particular subjects indicates that young migrants are happier taking photographs in places where they feel more at ease and less conspicuous, such as the home and the immediate neighbourhood. Is it possible that they felt that being seen in public with a large plastic camera would attract curiosity or unwanted (and unwelcome) attention? Could it be that they did not feel comfortable pointing a camera at white Italian people going about their business rather than consciously choosing subjects according to their relevance? Although it is difficult to verify, I believe that a concern with being exposed and conspicuous may have influenced the choice of subjects of the photographs, and that this concern can alter the images' significance.

I started to code the photographs taken by the children in Ghana, but since the participants I accessed all attended boarding schools, the limits of their physical setting meant that many of the images were very similar. The vast majority of these images, in contrast to the photographs taken in Italy, depicted people, in this case friends and classmates striking various poses, usually outside the same buildings – those that the children, as they later told me, were proud of. There were exceptions with some of the photographs depicting more unusual subjects, which gave interesting insights into the expectations of the young participants. But the vast majority were different angles of the same location, taken according to rules of attractiveness and propriety (Punch, 2002): fine buildings, well-tended flowery shrubs and grassy lawns.

> This is on the way to the XY block. I took the picture because I like the surroundings.
>
> Millisent, female, age 13, Ghana

Figure 8.3: Tree-lined street

These images are not without interest, as they reveal what the children found worthy of being preserved and shown to the white adult researcher who asked them to take photographs of their surroundings. When discussing the images during the individual interviews, the children fitted them into the briefing they were given: the similarities and differences between Ghana and Italy. However, I believe that considerations of propriety as well as spatial limitations probably influenced the choice of subjects, and that these influences needed to be considered at the analysis stage.

Whose eyes are we seeing through?

A further point for reflection specifically concerned my expectation that photographs could afford me a view of the world through the eyes of the young participants (Banks, 2007), and that away from my presence the children would be freer to choose what was really important to *them*. However, it became clear from the children's comments on the photographs that I was by no means absent when the images were taken. Having been asked to meet a specific brief, some of the children decided that the reality of their everyday surroundings was not real enough and that it needed a little help. Figure 8.4 and its accompanying comment exemplify this.

Wendibel wanted me to see images of dirt and waste dumping that concerned her and she believed would not be found in Italy. She admitted, however, that she and her friends had staged this picture, effectively creating the subject they wanted to photograph. Not only had she looked at her environment in the light of my briefing and found it wanting, but she had also involved her friends in the process, possibly discussing with them how to solve the problem of the 'unrealistic' cleanliness of her immediate surroundings.

Giovanna Fassetta

Figure 8.4: Staged dirt

> I snapped this because ... if I go to Italy I won't see this kind of thing ... This one ... Me and my friends, we did it ourselves, so that I could snap the picture. But people do it, but it's not good.
> Wendibel, female, age 13, Ghana

A similar process is apparent in Figure 8.5, which was taken by a young participant who was born in Italy:

Figure 8.5: Staged mess

> My cousin and I, since we wanted to take some African pictures, we threw everything in there ... In African rooms it's a mess ... especially families. Since we couldn't take an African family, we decided ...
> Roberto, male, age 14, Italy

Again, the participant had discussed the lack of a suitable subject with someone who was not directly involved in the research and decided to remedy reality's deficiency by staging something he wanted to portray. Both pictures exemplify the children's expectations and imaginings of the two countries and give an important insight into the narratives that inform these imaginings, as I had set out to investigate (Fassetta, 2011). However, it was clear that the participants had involved other people in taking the photographs and that the extent to which these people had influenced the resulting images could not be fully assessed. I was also clear that the participants had looked at their environment in the light of my request and had rectified it according to what they wished to show me or, perhaps, to what they anticipated a white Western researcher would expect to see. The researcher's 'absent presence' (Kesby, 2007) was unmistakable.

It is also recognizable in one of the photographs taken by Kate, an 11-year-old girl born in Italy of Ghanaian parents. The image portrays her living room, shelves filled with family pictures and ornamental objects. As Kate told me:

> I took this picture because these are all things that can be found in Ghana too. My parents told me that everything we have here can be found in Ghana too.

My request to photograph similarities and differences appears to have sparked a conversation with the family. Not only was my gaze perceptible in the picture, so was the gaze of the mother and father, who had looked at their surroundings through the white researcher's eyes and passed on their view to the child. The subject of the photographs was therefore the product of an ongoing conversation between the researcher, the participants and, at times, other individuals the children chose to involve (*cf.* Sime, 2008). In framing their pictures, the young participants' understanding of an adult Italian woman's gaze had combined with their own and sometimes also that of friends or family. The resulting images were, therefore, a 'composite picture', the product of a social interaction (Santoro and Smyth, 2010) rather than simply the point of view of the young participants. This is not so much a drawback of the technique as one that can afford important insights. However, assuming that the photographs directly reflect the participants' view of specific aspects of their lives may prove to be inaccurate or even misleading, and the possible conversations that might influence the images need to be openly acknowledged and included in the analysis to ensure that meanings are not misconstrued.

Photography and ethics: open issues

A significant concern when using child-led photography in research (Langevang, 2007) relates to the potential risks for a child holding a camera. Researchers need to be acutely aware of the possible difficulties the children may face when complying with our requests, such as derision, the irritation of unwilling subjects, or having the equipment stolen. However, young participants show that they are aware of such possibilities by keeping within the confines of safe places and actively reducing the chances of facing ridicule, or the risk of having the camera taken from them (ibid.). Restrictions on the potential location for the photographs – to ensure the safety that is rightly important – will influence the choice of subjects, and should be factored into the analysis and interpretation of the visual data.

Considerations of ethics and safety should, moreover, extend to the invasive potential that photography can have when children take cameras into their daily lives. The ethical grounds for intruding on individuals who are not directly involved in the research are questionable. Although the images taken were generally portraits of willing subjects who posed for a photo, some were 'stolen' moments of intimacy, and I found myself in the unanticipated position of a peeping Tom. One of the photographs showed a small child asleep in his cot. Another showed a father dozing on the sofa, another a pregnant woman scowling at the young photographer. These voyeuristic incursions into others' privacy may not be totally avoidable, or necessarily unethical, but they need to be included in the 'balance sheet' that informs the research design.

The children's views

The idea that photography is more attractive to young research participants because it is more fun (Clark-Ibáñez, 2007; Fassetta, 2010) also needs to be carefully considered. At the end of the individual interviews, I asked the children for feedback on the techniques they had used. When asked about whether they had enjoyed or disliked taking the photographs, about half of the participants told me they had not minded doing so. But the other half held polarized views on this: some considered it 'good fun' and even offered to take more photos, but an equivalent number viewed it as a chore they had resented having to do:

> GF: Was it a problem taking the photographs? Did you mind it?
> B: No. It was a pleasure! If you want I'll do some more [laughs].
>
> Benedetta, 12-year-old girl

> GF: Was taking the photographs a chore?
> M: Yes, a bit ... because you had to have a picture ... and you needed to think about it a lot, too.
>
> Marty, 12-year-old boy

Deciding what to photograph, striving to understand what it was that the researcher wanted from them, remembering to take the pictures, had all eaten into the children's free time and some were displeased. This could explain why a number of the photographs taken in Italy seemed to have been snapped in the space of a few minutes in the playground or classroom, and looked as though the children had dealt hurriedly with the task just before handing in the cameras.

The fact that the cameras were disposable may also have influenced the subjects of the photographs. Most of the children have digital cameras at home, whereas these were low-tech and possibly not something they were keen to be seen with. This was perhaps less of a problem in Ghana, as the participants were allowed to take photographs as a rare exception to otherwise strict school rules, and had therefore welcomed the privilege. However, taking photographs with disposable cameras requires a different technique to the one children associate with photography. Looking through a small viewfinder rather than a display, remembering to wind the film on, being unable to delete unwanted images, and having a limit on the number of exposures are all elements and limitations twenty-first-century children may not be used to, and may have influenced the visual data gathered.

Photography and empowerment

I am not implying that this technique is too fraught with difficulties and drawbacks to be effective. On the contrary, I argue that there are many benefits in the use of child-led photography. The major positive aspect of using it as a data collection technique can, however, make the researcher uncomfortable, as it requires them to relinquish control over the data collection process. That the children are not in the researcher's presence when they take pictures means that they are fully in charge of the output. While the subjects of the photographs may be chosen in light of a silent and ongoing conversation with the researcher, children can nevertheless resist, challenge, or even sabotage the researcher's requests: they can take a few hurried shots at the last minute; they can give the camera to others; they can say that the camera did not work so they could not take any pictures, as one of the participants in my project did. Photography allows children to portray something and retrospectively fit it into the research brief: they can remain silent by taking no photographs, or they can hijack the medium and take stills of elements they find interesting or photogenic. It is harder for young people to be as subversive when they are engaged face to face with an adult researcher.

Having control over the data collection process allows the participants real agency and begins to redress the imbalance of power embedded in adult–child interactions. But it also means that the researcher needs to deal with messy, complex data that may be difficult to analyse, since the subjects of the pictures cannot always be taken at face value. Discussing the photographs with the participants can help to clarify the dynamics that influence the choice of subjects, but the researcher still needs to engage with the technique reflexively (Pink, 2003) and assess and evaluate the likelihood that other factors may have influenced the children's choice of subjects (Kesby, 2007).

The photographs taken did provide an invaluable aid during the individual conversations. Using the images allowed the conversation to unfold around a structure the children had control over, as the images they had produced determined the conversation. They were also useful to direct attention away from the participants and thus allow for more relaxed interaction: eye contact could be avoided and awkward silences filled with detailed descriptions of the tangible objects. The conversation could move along freely, highlighting elements that might otherwise have been lost.

All techniques have their downsides: drawing can be awkward for children who do not see themselves as artistic; diaries can be unattractive for children who struggle with writing or with a new language; acting and role-play can be challenging for shy children. No single formula can be trusted to be right for everyone: personalities and individual preferences will always mean that using just one technique may result in someone feeling alienated, unsettled or jaded by the research process.

Using a multiple technique approach will increase the likelihood that all participants can find a medium through which they can express their thoughts, opinions and feelings (Barker and Weller, 2003; Darbyshire *et al.*, 2005). It allows for triangulation and the return of themes in different contexts and through different media, thus facilitating the emergence of strong themes and a deeper grounding of the interpretive process. A multiple technique approach and reflexive practice allows child-led photography to generate multifaceted insights.

Conclusion

Photography has grown increasingly popular as a tool for data collection, particularly with young people. While there is ample literature on the positive aspects of this technique, its potential drawbacks are less thoroughly discussed. Like other techniques, child-led photography does not guarantee that children will be actively engaged in the research process, nor can it ensure that they will photograph the world as they see it. Photographs are neither still nor silent; looked at from a reflexive standpoint they are a product of the dynamic, ongoing interaction between several people. However little input the researcher makes, it may subtly change the way the participants look at their world. The act of holding a camera impacts on the way we view our surroundings: reality becomes something to be framed and immortalized, and not everything can be captured, so choices have to be made (Goldstein, 2007). In addition to the photographs taken, there are all those that were not taken; what is avoided may be as revealing as what is portrayed.

The photographs taken by children can offer insights into the way in which young people look at their experiences and surroundings when stimulated by the brief of the research. In my study, several of the photographs contained much information about the children's expectations of what might interest a white Italian researcher, as well as about the dynamics of interaction between the absent researcher and the present others in their lives. Building these insights into the design of a project; encouraging the conversation rather than trying to prevent it; evaluating the data as a choral performance to which many have contributed, rather than the expression of one individual's point of view: these are all practices that can ensure that a potential weakness becomes a strength.

The fact that children may not wish to take photographs in public places or may feel shy about attracting attention by pointing a camera needs to be considered when looking at the images. Determining when and where the use of child-led photography is appropriate and giving the cameras to groups rather than individuals would recognize and exploit the joint nature of the technique and help the children to feel less vulnerable when taking photos (Catts *et al.*, 2007). Giving participants the chance to alter the images manually or, to manipulate digital images using software allows them to rectify elements they are not happy with, and shape the images to expose what they intended more fully (ibid.). Creating group posters or slideshows with the images and discussing other groups' creations can involve the children in the analysis of the visual data.

To understand the young photographers' intentions and to gain an insight into the processes that have led to their choices, they must be given opportunities to comment on their photographs. The oral or written text accompanying an image can form an integral unit, anchoring the image, highlighting the elements of particular relevance, and operating as a 'relay', the starting point of a complementary narrative (Barthes, 1999).

This chapter contributes to a critical appraisal of the use of children's photographs for research. The benefits, peculiarities and drawbacks of the technique are outlined, so that it can be chosen in full awareness of what it allows and what it may preclude or distort. I have explored the grounds on which visual data can be analysed: by acknowledging the data as a 'choral' endeavour that engages at least two people in conversation; and by recognizing the social dynamics and processes that take place in the making of an image.

References

Banks, M. (2007) *Using Visual Data in Qualitative Research*. London: Sage.
Barker, J. and Weller, S. (2003) '"Is it fun?" Developing children centred research methods'. *International Journal of Sociology and Social Policy*, 23 (1/2), 33–58.

Barthes, R. (1999) 'Rhetoric of the image'. In Evans, J. and Hall, S. (eds) *Visual Culture: The reader*. London: Sage, 33–40.

Catts, R., Allan, J. and Smyth, G. (2007) 'Children's Voices: How do we address their right to be heard?'. *Scottish Educational Review*, 39 (1), 51–9.

Clark, A. (2010) 'Young children as protagonists and the role of participatory, visual methods in engaging multiple perspectives'. *Community Psychology*, 46, 115–23.

Clark-Ibáñez, M. (2007) 'Inner-city children in sharper focus: Sociology of childhood and photo elicitation interviews'. In Stanczak, G.C. (ed.) *Visual Research Methods: Image, society and representation*. London: Sage, 167–96.

Crenshaw, K. (1991) 'Mapping the Margins: Intersectionality, identity politics and violence against women of color'. *Stanford Law Review*, 43, 1241–99.

Darbyshire, P., MacDougall, C. and Schiller, W. (2005) 'Multiple methods in qualitative research with children: More insight or just more?' *Qualitative Research*, 5, 417–36.

Dodman, D.R. (2003) 'Shooting in the city: An autophotographic exploration of the urban environment in Kingston, Jamaica'. *Area*, 35 (3): 293–304.

Enright, E. and O'Sullivan, M. (2012) '"Producing different knowledge and producing knowledge differently": Rethinking physical education research through participatory visual methods'. *Sport, Education and Society*, 17 (1): 35–55.

Fassetta, G. (2010) 'Without a safety net: Participatory techniques in research with young migrants'. *Enquire*, 3 (1), 95–116.

— (2011) '"It's beautiful. That's why we call it abroad". Migrant Children's imaginings and expectations of migration.' PhD thesis, University of Strathclyde.

— (2013) 'Communicating attitudes. Ghanaian children's expectations and experiences of Italian educational institutions.' *Childhood*. Published online before print (subscription required). http://chd.sagepub.com/content/early/2013/12/02/0907568213512691.abstract (published 4 December).

Gallacher, L.A. and Gallagher, M. (2008) 'Methodological immaturity in childhood research? Thinking through "participatory methods"'. *Childhood*, 15 (4), 499–516.

Gallagher, M. (2008) '"Power is not an evil": Rethinking power in participatory methods'. *Children's Geographies*, 6 (2), 137–50.

Goldstein, B.M. (2007) 'All photos lie: Images as data'. In Stanczak, G.C. (ed.) *Visual Research Methods: Image, society and representation*. London: Sage, 61–81.

Holloway, S.L. and Valentine, G. (eds) (2000) *Children's Geographies: Playing, living, learning*. London: Routledge.

James, A. and James, A. (2004) *Constructing Childhood: Theory, policy and social practice*. Basingstoke: Palgrave Macmillan.

James, A. (2007) 'Giving voice to children's voices: Practices and problems, pitfalls and potentials'. *American Anthropologist*, 109 (2), 261–72.

Kesby, M. (2007) 'Methodological insights on and from children's geographies'. *Children's Geographies*, 5 (3), 93–205.

Kothari, U. (2001) 'Power, knowledge and social control in participatory development'. In Cooke, B. and Kothari, U. (eds) *Participation: The new tyranny?* London: Zed Books, 139–53.

Langevang, T. (2007) 'Movements in time and space: Using multiple methods in research with young people in Accra, Ghana'. *Children's Geographies*, 5 (3), 267–81.

Morgan, M., Gibbs, S., Maxwell, K. and Britten, N. (2002) 'Hearing children's voices: methodological issues in conducting focus groups with children aged 7–11 years'. *Qualitative Research*, 2 (1), 5–20.

Nash, J.C. (2008) 'Re-thinking intersectionality'. *Feminist Review*, 89: 1–15.

Oh, S.A. (2012) 'Photofriend: Creating visual ethnography with refugee children'. *Area*, 44 (3), 282–8.

Ortega-Alcázar, I. and Dyck, I. (2012) 'Migrant narratives of health and well-being: Challenging "othering" processes through photo-elicitation interviews'. *Critical Social Policy*, 32 (1), 106–25.

Pink, S. (2003) 'Interdisciplinary agendas in visual research: Re-situating visual anthropology'. *Visual Studies*, 18 (2), 179–92.

Punch, S. (2002) 'Research with children. The same or different from research with adults?' *Childhood*, 9 (3), 321–41.

Santoro, N. and Smyth, G. (2010) 'Researching ethnic "others": conducting critical ethnographic research in Australia and Scotland'. *Intercultural Education*, 21 (6), 493–503.

Said, E. (1978) *Orientalism*. London: Penguin.

Sharples, M., Davison, L., Thomas, G.V. and Rudman, P. (2003) 'Children as photographers: An analysis of children's photographic behaviour and intentions at three age levels'. *Visual Communications*, 23 (3), 303–30.

Sime, D. (2008) 'Ethical and methodological issues in involving young people living in poverty with participatory research methods'. *Children's Geographies*, 6 (1), 63–78.

Spivak, G.C. (1988) 'Can the subaltern speak?' In Nelson, C. and Grossberg L. (eds) *Marxism and the Interpretation of Culture*. Basingstoke: Macmillan Education, 271–313.

Suárez-Orozco, C. and Suárez-Orozco, M.M. (2001) *Children of Immigration*. Cambridge, MA: Harvard University Press.

Tisdall, E.K.M. and Punch, S. (2012) 'Not so "new"? Looking critically at childhood studies'. *Children's Geographies*, 10 (3), 249–64.

Young, L. and Barrett, H. (2001) 'Adapting visual methods: Action research with Kampala street children'. *Area*, 33 (2), 141–52.

Index

action research   15–22, 91–105
Australia   26–41, 75–90;

Banks, M.   106, 113
Butler, J.   29, 33–5, 37, 41

Canada   14–25, 91–105
Clarke, A.   76–8, 86, 88–9
collaborative research   15, 18, 20
constructing maps   77
critical analysis   38
critical participatory action research   15–19, 23
critical reflection   47
cultural outsiders   xiii, xv, 54, 89
Cummins, J.   xiv, 60–1, 69, 72, 96–7

Denscombe, N.   44, 46, 49–50, 55
discursive shadowing   1–2, 5–7, 10–11

empowering research   60
ethics   2, 6, 8–11, 20–4, 45–6, 98, 115
ethnographic data   31
ethnography   27–8, 32

focus group   17–19, 68, 110

Ghana   106–21

human elements   77

insider/outsider positioning   19
insider-researcher   42–50, 52
interviews   5, 9–10, 31, 41, 44–7, 49–55, 67–8, 70, 74–5, 77–8, 88, 95, 109, 110, 113, 116
Italy   106–21

Jirón, P.   6–7, 10

Kincheloe, J.   16–17, 23–24

Langevang, T.   106, 108, 110, 115
Lee, E. and Simon-Maeda, A.   18–19, 23–4
longitudinal case study   75
longitudinal interview data   75
longitudinal research   15, 88

McDonald, S.   5–6
Meleis, A.I.   59, 61, 69
messy map   78, 81–3
messy situational map   78–9
Morrison, M.   45, 47, 56

narrative   26, 30, 32–3, 35, 49, 69, 75, 78, 93, 100, 107, 114, 119
non-human elements   77
Norway   1–13

observation   28–9, 31
open space technology   58, 62, 64
outsider-researcher   42–4, 54

Pakistan   42–57
participant positionality   16
participatory action research   xiii–xiv, 15–19, 21, 23, 91–6, 100, 102–04
participatory research   16, 58, 68
pedagogical orientations   96–7
photography   xv, 58, 69, 106–21
positionalities of researchers   43
post-structural ethnography   xiv, 26–9, 38
power   x, xiv–xv, 8, 10–11, 16, 18, 22, 26, 30, 32, 34, 36, 38, 42–3, 50–1, 55, 58–9, 61, 64, 68, 70–2, 87, 91, 95–6, 99, 102–03, 106–09, 117
practitioner research   15

reflexivity   18, 30, 47–8
relational map   78, 83–6
research questions   59–60, 69, 101
researcher positioning   19, 74

Scotland   58–73
semi-structured interview   9–10, 31, 67, 74
situational analysis   xv, 77–8, 88–9, 75–90
situational map   78–9, 81–2
social justice   ix–x, xiii, 27, 38, 58, 89
social worlds/arenas map   78, 86, 89
socio-professional insider   43
subjectivities   29–30, 35, 38, 42, 44, 47

teacher-researcher   17–20

Youdell, D.   27, 41